SELECTED POEMS

BY

WALT WHITMAN

New York
CHARLES L. WEBSTER & CO.
1892

PRESS OF
JENKINS & McCOWAN,
NEW YORK.

EDITOR'S NOTE

THIS edition of Mr. Whitman's poems is, on his part,
a concession to friendship. He has not abandoned his
position, but has yielded to urgent request. Several
eclectic editions of "Leaves of Grass" have been issued in England and Scotland, most of them with his
half-willing consent. Here, where he can assert his
rights, he never has permitted one such to appear.

With regard to the editor, the volume is partially a
concession to the spirit which banished "Leaves of
Grass" from Massachusetts. It cannot, however, be
styled a concession to the New England critics who
begrudge any good thing which comes out of Manhattan. It is intended rather as a justification of New
England's leaders of thought, who have consistently
appreciated Mr. Whitman's genius from the first.

My intention has been to offer, in a conventional
form, those of his poems which are held to be most
nearly in harmony with the poetic era (though really
they have a character quite apart from it), and to add
selections from his more distinctive chantings. With
the choice and arrangement of the poems Mr. Whitman has had nothing to do, save in the most general
way of approval.

I sincerely believe this little collection will be a revelation even to those who know their Whitman. It seems to me that a defective lyrical sense can be the only excuse for those who do not find him wonderfully rhythmic. Some may declare that I have tried to chisel a statuette out of a particularly rugged boulder, but if they will admit that the carving has been neatly done, they are welcome to call the book a paradox.

CONTENTS

NATURE, MAN, AND SELF

TO THE MAN-OF-WAR-BIRD

Thou who hast slept all night upon the storm,
Waking renew'd on thy prodigious pinions,
(Burst the wild storm? above it thou ascended'st,
And rested on the sky, thy slave that cradled thee,)
Now a blue point, far, far in heaven floating,
As to the light emerging here on deck I watch thee,
(Myself a speck, a point on the world's floating vast.)

Far, far at sea,
After the night's fierce drifts have strewn the shore with
    wrecks,
With re-appearing day as now so happy and serene,
The rosy and elastic dawn, the flashing sun,
The limpid spread of air cerulean,
Thou also re-appearest.

Thou born to match the gale, (thou art all wings,)
To cope with heaven and earth and sea and hurricane,
Thou ship of air that never furl'st thy sails,
Days, even weeks untired and onward, through spaces,
    realms gyrating,
At dusk that look'st on Senegal, at morn America,
That sport'st amid the lightning-flash and thunder-cloud,
In them, in thy experiences, had'st thou my soul,
What joys! what joys were thine!

A PAUMANOK PICTURE

Two boats with nets lying off the sea-beach, quite still.
Ten fishermen waiting—they discover a thick school of
    mossbonkers—they drop the join'd seine-ends in the
    water,
The boats separate and row off, each on its rounding course
    to the beach, enclosing the mossbonkers,
The net is drawn in by a windlass by those who stop ashore,
Some of the fishermen lounge in their boats, others stand
    ankle-deep in the water, pois'd on strong legs,
The boats partly drawn up, the water slapping against
    them,
Strew'd on the sand in heaps and windrows, well out from
    the water, the green-back'd spotted mossbonkers.

PATROLING BARNEGAT

WILD, wild the storm, and the sea high running,
Steady the roar of the gale, with incessant undertone mut-
    tering,
Shouts of demoniac laughter fitfully piercing and pealing,
Waves, air, midnight, their savagest trinity lashing,
Out in the shadows there milk-white combs careering,
On beachy slush and sand spirts of snow fierce slanting,
Where through the murk the easterly death-wind breasting,
Through cutting swirl and spray watchful and firm advan-
    cing,
(That in the distance! is that a wreck? is the red signal
    flaring?)

Slush and sand of the beach tireless till daylight wending,
Steadily, slowly, through hoarse roar never remitting,
Along the midnight edge by those milk-white combs career-
    ing,
A group of dim, weird forms, struggling, the night con-
    fronting,
That savage trinity warily watching.

WITH HUSKY-HAUGHTY LIPS, O SEA !

WITH husky-haughty lips, O sea !
Where day and night I wend thy surf-beat shore,
Imaging to my sense thy varied strange suggestions,
(I see and plainly list thy talk and conference here,)
Thy troops of white-maned racers racing to the goal,
Thy ample, smiling face, dash'd with the sparkling dimples
        of the sun,
Thy brooding scowl and murk—thy unloos'd hurricanes,
Thy unsubduedness, caprices, wilfulness;
Great as thou art above the rest, thy many tears—a lack
        from all eternity in thy content,
(Naught but the greatest struggles, wrongs, defeats, could
        make thee greatest—no less could make thee,)
Thy lonely state—something thou ever seek'st and seek'st,
        yet never gain'st,
Surely some right withheld—some voice, in huge monoto-
        nous rage, of freedom-lover pent,
Some vast heart, like a planet's, chain'd and chafing in those
        breakers,
By lengthen'd swell, and spasm, and panting breath,
And rhythmic rasping of thy sands and waves,
And serpent hiss, and savage peals of laughter,
And undertones of distant lion roar,
(Sounding, appealing to the sky's deaf ear—but now, rapport
        for once,
A phantom in the night thy confidant for once,)
The first and last confession of the globe,
Outsurging, muttering from thy soul's abysms,
The tale of cosmic elemental passion,
Thou tellest to a kindred soul.

OLD SALT KOSSABONE

FAR back, related on my mother's side,
Old Salt Kossabone, I'll tell you how he died:
(Had been a sailor all his life—was nearly 90—lived with
     his married grandchild, Jenny;
House on a hill, with view of bay at hand, and distant
     cape, and stretch to open sea;)
The last of afternoons, the evening hours, for many a year
     his regular custom,
In his great arm chair by the window seated,
(Sometimes, indeed, through half the day,)
Watching the coming, going of the vessels, he mutters to
     himself
     —And now the close of all:
One struggling outbound brig, one day, baffled for long—
     cross-tides and much wrong going,
At last at nightfall strikes the breeze aright, her whole luck
     veering,
And swiftly bending round the cape, the darkness proudly
     entering, cleaving, as he watches,
" She's free—she's on her destination "—these the last
     words—when Jenny came, he sat there dead,
Dutch Kossabone, Old Salt, related on my mother's side,
     far back.

TO THE SUN-SET BREEZE

AH, whispering, something again, unseen,
Where late this heated day thou enterest at my window,
    door,
Thou, laving, tempering all, cool-freshing, gently vitaliz-
    ing
Me, old, alone, sick, weak-down, melted-worn with sweat;
Thou, nestling, folding close and firm yet soft, companion
    better than talk, book, art,
(Thou hast, O Nature! elements! utterance to my heart
    beyond the rest—and this is of them,)
So sweet thy primitive taste to breathe within—thy sooth-
    ing fingers on my face and hands,
Thou, messenger-magical strange bringer to body and
    spirit of me,
(Distances balk'd—occult medicines penetrating me from
    head to foot,)
I feel the sky, the prairies vast—I feel the mighty northern
    lakes,
I feel the ocean and the forest—somehow I feel the globe
    itself swift-swimming in space;
Thou blown from lips so loved, now gone—haply from end-
    less store, God-sent,
(For thou art spiritual, Godly, most of all known to my
    sense,)
Minister to speak to me, here and now, what word has
    never told, and cannot tell,
Art thou not universal concrete's distillation? Law's all
    Astronomy's last refinement?
Hast thou no soul? Can I not know, identify thee?

FROM FAR DAKOTA'S CAÑONS

(*June* 25, 1876)

FROM far Dakota's cañons,
Lands of the wild ravine, the dusky Sioux, the lonesome
    stretch, the silence,
Haply to-day a mournful wail, haply a trumpet-note for
    heroes.

The battle-bulletin,
The Indian ambuscade, the craft, the fatal environment,
The cavalry companies fighting to the last in sternest
    heroism,
In the midst of their little circle, with their slaughter'd
    horses for breastworks,
The fall of Custer and all his officers and men.

Continues yet the old, old legend of our race,
The loftiest of life upheld by death,
The ancient banner perfectly maintain'd,
O lesson opportune, O how I welcome thee !

As sitting in dark days,
Lone, sulky, through the time's thick murk looking in
    vain for light, for hope,
From unsuspected parts a fierce and momentary proof,
(The sun there at the centre though conceal'd,
Electric life forever at the centre,)
Breaks forth a lightning flash.

Thou of the tawny flowing hair in battle,
I erewhile saw, with erect head, pressing ever in front,
    bearing a bright sword in thy hand,
Now ending well in death the splendid fever of thy deeds,
(I bring no dirge for it or thee, I bring a glad triumphal
    sonnet,)
Desperate and glorious, aye in defeat most desperate,
    most glorious,
After thy many battles in which never yielding up a gun
    or a color,
Leaving behind thee a memory sweet to soldiers,
Thou yieldest up thyself.

DEATH OF GENERAL GRANT

As one by one withdraw the lofty actors,
From that great play on history's stage eterne,
That lurid, partial act of war and peace—of old and new
    contending,
Fought out through wrath, fears, dark dismays, and many
    a long suspense;
All past—and since, in countless graves receding, mellow-
    ing,
Victor's and vanquish'd—Lincoln's and Lee's—now thou
    with them,
Man of the mighty days—and equal to the days!
Thou from the prairies!—tangled and many-vein'd and
    hard has been thy part,
To admiration has it been enacted!

THE DEAD TENOR

As down the stage again,
With Spanish hat and plumes, and gait inimitable,
Back from the fading lessons of the past, I'd call, I'd tell
      and own,
How much from thee! the revelation of the singing voice
      from thee!
(So firm—so liquid-soft—again that tremulous, manly
      timbre!
The perfect singing voice—deepest of all to me the lesson
      —trial and test of all:)
How through those strains distill'd—how the rapt ears, the
      soul of me, absorbing
Fernando's heart, *Manrico's* passionate call, *Ernani's*, sweet
      Gennaro's,
I fold thenceforth, or seek to fold, within my chants trans-
      muting,
Freedom's and Love's and Faith's unloos'd cantabile,
(As perfume's, color's, sunlight's correlation:)
From these, for these, with these, a hurried line, dead
      tenor,
A wafted autumn leaf, dropt in the closing grave, the
      shovel'd earth,
To memory of thee.

PRAYER OF COLUMBUS

A BATTER'D, wreck'd old man,
Thrown on this savage shore, far, far from home,
Pent by the sea and dark rebellious brows, twelve dreary
    months,
Sore, stiff with many toils, sicken'd and nigh to death,
I take my way along the island's edge,
Venting a heavy heart.

I am too full of woe !
Haply I may not live another day ;
I cannot rest O God, I cannot eat or drink or sleep,
Till I put forth myself, my prayer, once more to Thee,
Breathe, bathe myself once more in Thee, commune with
    Thee,
Report myself once more to Thee.

Thou knowest my years entire, my life,
My long and crowded life of active work, not adoration
    merely;
Thou knowest the prayers and vigils of my youth,
Thou knowest my manhood's solemn and visionary med-
    itations,
Thou knowest how before I commenced I devoted all to
    come to Thee,
Thou knowest I have in age ratified all those vows and
    strictly kept them,
Thou knowest I have not once lost nor faith nor ecstasy in
    Thee.

In shackles, prison'd, in disgrace, repining not,
Accepting all from Thee, as duly come from Thee.

All my emprises have been fill'd with Thee,
My speculations, plans, begun and carried on in thoughts
    of Thee,
Sailing the deep or journeying the land for Thee;
Intentions, purports, aspirations mine, leaving results to
    Thee.

O I am sure they really came from Thee,
The urge, the ardor, the unconquerable will,
The potent, felt, interior command, stronger than words,
A message from the Heavens whispering to me even in sleep,
These sped me on.

By me and these the work so far accomplish'd,
By me earth's elder cloy'd and stifled lands uncloy'd, un-
    loos'd,
By me the hemispheres rounded and tied, the unknown to
    the known.

The end I know not, it is all in Thee,
Or small or great I know not—haply what broad fields, what
    lands,
Haply the brutish measureless human undergrowth I know,
Transplanted there may rise to stature, knowledge worthy
    Thee,
Haply the swords I know may there be turn'd to reaping-
    tools,
Haply the lifeless cross I know, Europe's dead cross, may
    bud and blossom there.

One effort more, my altar this bleak sand;
That Thou O God my life hast lighted,
With ray of light, steady, ineffable, vouchsafed of Thee,
Light rare untellable, lighting the very light,
Beyond all signs, descriptions, languages;
For that O God, be it my latest word, here on my knees,
Old, poor, and paralyzed, I thank Thee.

My terminus near,
The clouds already closing in upon me,
The voyage balk'd, the course disputed, lost,
I yield my ships to Thee.

My hands, my limbs grow nerveless,
My brain feels rack'd, bewilder'd,
Let the old timbers part, I will not part,
I will cling fast to Thee, O God, though the waves buffet me,
Thee, Thee at least I know.

Is it the prophet's thought I speak, or am I raving?
What do I know of life? what of myself?
I know not even my own work past or present,
Dim ever-shifting guesses of it spread before me,
Of newer better worlds, their mighty parturition,
Mocking, perplexing me.

And these things I see suddenly, what mean they?
As if some miracle, some hand divine unseal'd my eyes,
Shadowy vast shapes smile through the air and sky,
And on the distant waves sail countless ships,
And anthems in new tongues I hear saluting me.

OLD IRELAND

FAR hence amid an isle of wondrous beauty,
Crouching over a grave an ancient sorrowful mother,
Once a queen, now lean and tatter'd seated on the ground,
Her old white hair drooping dishevel'd round her shoulders,
At her feet fallen an unused royal harp,
Long silent, she too long silent, mourning her shrouded
    hope and heir,
Of all the earth her heart most full of sorrow because most
    full of love.

Yet a word ancient mother,
You need crouch there no longer on the cold ground with
    forehead between your knees,
O you need not sit there veil'd in your old white hair so
    dishevel'd,
For know you the one you mourn is not in that grave,
It was an illusion, the son you love was not really dead,
The Lord is not dead, he is risen again young and strong in
    another country,
Even while you wept there by your fallen harp by the grave,
What you wept for was translated, pass'd from the grave,
The winds favor'd and the sea sail'd it,
And now with rosy and new blood,
Moves to-day in a new country.

O STAR OF FRANCE

(1870-71)

O STAR of France,
The brightness of thy hope and strength and fame,
Like some proud ship that led the fleet so long,
Beseems to-day a wreck driven by the gale, a mastless
    hulk,
And 'mid its teeming madden'd half-drown'd crowds,
Nor helm nor helmsman.

Dim smitten star,
Orb not of France alone, pale symbol of my soul, its dear-
    est hopes,
The struggle and the daring, rage divine for liberty,
Of aspirations toward the far ideal, enthusiast's dreams of
    brotherhood,
Of terror to the tyrant and the priest.

Star crucified—by traitors sold,
Star panting o'er a land of death, heroic land,
Strange, passionate, mocking, frivolous land.

Miserable! yet for thy errors, vanities, sins, I will not
    now rebuke thee,
Thy unexampled woes and pangs have quell'd them all,
And left thee sacred.

In that amid thy many faults thou ever aimedst highly,
In that thou wouldst not really sell thyself however great
    the price,

In that thou surely wakedst weeping from thy drugg'd
    sleep,
In that alone among thy sisters thou, giantess, didst rend
    the ones that shamed thee,
In that thou couldst not, wouldst not, wear the usual
    chains,
This cross, thy livid face, thy pierced hands and feet,
The spear thrust in thy side.

O star! O ship of France, beat back and baffled long!
Bear up O smitten orb!   O ship continue on!

Sure as the ship of all, the Earth itself,
Product of deathly fire and turbulent chaos,
Forth from its spasms of fury and its poisons,
Issuing at last in perfect power and beauty,
Onward beneath the sun following its course,
So thee O ship of France!

Finish'd the days, the clouds dispel'd,
The travail o'er, the long-sought extrication,
When lo! reborn, high o'er the European world,
(In gladness answering thence, as face afar to face, reflect-
    ing ours Columbia,)
Again thy star O France, fair lustrous star,
In heavenly peace, clearer, more bright than ever,
Shall beam immortal.

THE JUSTIFIED MOTHER OF MEN

THE old face of the mother of many children,
Whist! I am fully content.

Lull'd and late is the smoke of the First-day morning,
It hangs low over the rows of trees by the fences,
It hangs thin by the sassafras and wild-cherry and cat-brier
    under them.
I saw the rich ladies in full dress at the soiree,
I heard what the singers were singing so long,
Heard who sprang in crimson youth from the white froth
    and the water-blue.

Behold a woman!
She looks out from her quaker cap, her face is clearer and
    more beautiful than the sky.

She sits in an armchair under the shaded porch of the farm-
    house,
The sun just shines on her old white head.

Her ample gown is of cream-hued linen,
Her grandsons raised the flax, and her grand-daughters
    spun it with the distaff and the wheel.

The melodious character of the earth,
The finish beyond which philosophy cannot go and does
    not wish to go,
The justified mother of men.

SPIRIT THAT FORM'D THIS SCENE

(*Written in Platte Cañon, Colorado*)

SPIRIT that form'd this scene,
These tumbled rock-piles grim and red,
These reckless heaven-ambitious peaks,
These gorges, turbulent-clear streams, this naked fresh-
    ness,
These formless wild arrays, for reasons of their own,
I know thee, savage spirit—we have communed together,
Mine too such wild arrays, for reasons of their own;
Was't charged against my chants they had forgotten art?
To fuse within themselves its rules precise and delicatesse?
The lyrist's measur'd beat, the wrought-out temple's
    grace—column and polish'd arch forgot?
But thou that revelest here—spirit that form'd this scene,
They have remember'd thee.

WHEN I HEARD THE LEARN'D ASTRONOMER

WHEN I heard the learn'd astronomer,
When the proofs, the figures, were ranged in columns be-
    fore me,
When I was shown the charts and diagrams, to add, divide,
    and measure them,
When I sitting heard the astronomer where he lectured
    with much applause in the lecture-room,
How soon unaccountable I became tired and sick,
Till rising and gliding out I wander'd off by myself,
In the mystical moist night-air, and from time to time,
Look'd up in perfect silence at the stars.

OUT FROM BEHIND THIS MASK

(To Confront a Portrait)

I

OUT from behind this bending rough-cut mask,
These lights and shades, this drama of the whole,
This common curtain of the face contain'd in me for me, in
    you for you, in each for each,
(Tragedies, sorrows, laughter, tears—O heaven!
The passionate teeming plays this curtain hid!)
This glaze of God's serenest purest sky,
This film of Satan's seething pit,
This heart's geography's map, this limitless small conti-
    nent, this soundless sea;
Out from the convolutions of this globe,
This subtler astronomic orb than sun or moon, than Jupi-
    ter, Venus, Mars,
This condensation of the universe, (nay here the only uni-
    verse,
Here the idea, all in this mystic handful wrapt;)
These burin'd eyes, flashing to you to pass to future time,
To launch and spin through space revolving sideling, from
    these to emanate,
To you whoe'er you are—a look.

2

A traveler of thoughts and years, of peace and war,
Of youth long sped and middle age declining,

(As the first volume of a tale perused and laid away, and
    this the second,
Songs, ventures, speculations, presently to close,)
Lingering a moment here and now, to you I opposite turn,
As on the road or at some crevice door by chance, or
    open'd window,
Pausing, inclining, baring my head, you specially I greet,
To draw and clinch your soul for once inseparably with
    mine,
Then travel travel on.

RECORDERS AGES HENCE

RECORDERS ages hence,
Come, I will take you down underneath this impassive ex-
    terior, I will tell you what to say of me,
Publish my name and hang up my picture as that of the
    tenderest lover.
The friend the lover's portrait, of whom his friend his lover
    was fondest,
Who was not proud of his songs, but of the measureless
    ocean of love within him, and freely pour'd it forth,
Who often walk'd lonesome walks thinking of his dear
    friends, his lovers,
Who pensive away from one he lov'd often lay sleepless
    and dissatisfied at night,
Who knew too well the sick, sick dread lest the one he
    lov'd might secretly be indifferent to him,
Whose happiest days were far away through fields, in
    woods, on hills, he and another wandering hand in
    hand, they twain apart from other men,
Who oft as he saunter'd the streets curv'd with his arm the
    shoulder of his friend, while the arm of his friend rested
    upon him also.

BY BROAD POTOMAC'S SHORE

By broad Potomac's shore, again old tongue,
(Still uttering, still ejaculating, canst never cease this bab-
    ble?)
Again old heart so gay, again to you, your sense, the full
    flush spring returning,
Again the freshness and the odors, again Virginia's sum-
    mer sky, pellucid blue and silver,
Again the forenoon purple of the hills,
Again the deathless grass, so noiseless soft and green,
Again the blood-red roses blooming.

Perfume this book of mine O blood-red roses!
Lave subtly with your waters every line Potomac!
Give me of you O spring, before I close, to put between its
    pages!
O forenoon purple of the hills, before I close, of you!
O deathless grass, of you!

INTERLUDES

THE MYSTIC TRUMPETER

1

HARK, some wild trumpeter, some strange musician,
Hovering unseen in air, vibrates capricious tunes to-night.

I hear thee trumpeter, listening alert I catch thy notes,
Now pouring, whirling like a tempest round me,
Now low, subdued, now in the distance lost.

2

Come nearer bodiless one, haply in thee resounds
Some dead composer, haply thy pensive life ⁻
Was fill'd with aspirations high, unform'd ideals,
Waves, oceans musical, chaotically surging,
That now ecstatic ghost, close to me bending, thy cornet
    echoing, pealing,
Gives out to no one's ears but mine, but freely gives to
    mine,
That I may thee translate.

3

Blow trumpeter free and clear, I follow thee,
While at thy liquid prelude, glad, serene,
The fretting world, the streets, the noisy hours of day
    withdraw,
A holy calm descends like dew upon me,
I walk in cool refreshing night the walks of Paradise,
I scent the grass, the moist air and the roses;

Thy song expands my numb'd imbonded spirit, thou freest,
    launchest me,
Floating and basking upon heaven's lake.

4

Blow again trumpeter! and for my sensuous eyes,
Bring the old pageants, show the feudal world.

What charm thy music works! thou makest pass before me,
Ladies and cavaliers long dead, barons are in their castle
    halls, the troubadours are singing,
Arm'd knights go forth to redress wrongs, some in quest
    of the holy Graal;
I see the tournament, I see the contestants incased in
    heavy armor seated on stately champing horses,
I hear the shouts, the sounds of blows and smiting steel;
I see the Crusaders' tumultuous armies — hark, how the
    cymbals clang,
Lo, where the monks walk in advance, bearing the cross on
    high.

5

Blow again trumpeter! and for thy theme,
Take now the enclosing theme of all, the solvent and the
    setting,
Love, that is pulse of all, the sustenance and the pang,
The heart of man and woman all for love,
No other theme but love—knitting, enclosing, all-diffusing
    love.

O how the immortal phantoms crowd around me!
I see the vast alembic ever working, I see and know the
    flames that heat the world,
The glow, the blush, the beating hearts of lovers,

So blissful happy some, and some so silent, dark, and nigh
    to death;
Love, that is all the earth to lovers—love, that mocks time
    and space,
Love, that is day and night—love, that is sun and moon
    and stars,
Love, that is crimson, sumptuous, sick with perfume,
No other words but words of love, no other thought but
    love.

6

Blow again trumpeter—conjure war's alarums.

Swift to thy spell a shuddering hum like distant thunder
    rolls,
Lo, where the arm'd men hasten—lo, mid the clouds of
    dust the glint of bayonets,
I see the grime-faced cannoneers, I mark the rosy flash
    amid the smoke, I hear the cracking of the guns;
Nor war alone—thy fearful music-song, wild player, brings
    every sight of fear,
The deeds of ruthless brigands, rapine, murder—I hear the
    cries for help!
I see ships foundering at sea, I behold on deck and below
    deck the terrible tableaus.

7

O trumpeter, methinks I am myself the instrument thou
    playest,
Thou melt'st my heart, my brain—thou movest, drawest,
    changest them at will;
And now thy sullen notes send darkness through me,
Thou takest away all cheering light, all hope,

I see the enslaved, the overthrown, the hurt, the opprest of
    the whole earth,
I feel the measureless shame and humiliation of my race, it
    becomes all mine,
Mine too the revenges of humanity, the wrongs of ages,
    baffled feuds and hatreds,
Utter defeat upon me weighs—all lost—the foe victorious,
(Yet 'mid the ruins Pride colossal stands unshaken to the
    last,
Endurance, resolution to the last.)

8

Now trumpeter for thy close,
Vouchsafe a higher strain than any yet,
Sing to my soul, renew its languishing faith and hope,
Rouse up my slow belief, give me some vision of the future,
Give me for once its prophecy and joy.

O glad, exulting, culminating song!
A vigor more than earth's is in thy notes,
Marches of victory—man disenthral'd—the conqueror at
    last,
Hymns to the universal God from universal man—all joy!
A reborn race appears—a perfect world, all joy!
Women and men in wisdom innocence and health—all joy!
Riotous laughing bacchanals fill'd with joy!
War, sorrow, suffering gone—the rank earth purged—noth-
    ing but joy left!
The ocean fill'd with joy—the atmosphere all joy!
Joy! joy! in freedom, worship, love! joy in the ecstasy of
    life!
Enough to merely be! enough to breathe!
Joy! joy! all over joy!

FROM ''OUT OF THE CRADLE ENDLESSLY
ROCKING ''

ONCE Paumanok,
When the lilac-scent was in the air and Fifth-month grass
    was growing,
Up this seashore in some briers,
Two feather'd guests from Alabama, two together,
And their nest, and four light-green eggs spotted with
    brown,
And every day the he-bird to and fro near at hand,
And every day the she-bird crouch'd on her nest, silent,
    with bright eyes,
And every day I, a curious boy, never too close, never dis-
    turbing them,
Cautiously peering, absorbing, translating.

Shine ! shine ! shine !
Pour down your warmth, great sun !
While we bask, we two together.

Two together !
Winds blow south, or winds blow`north,
Day come white, or night come black,
Home, or rivers and mountains from home,
Singing all time, minding no time,
While we two keep together.

Till of a sudden,
May-be killed, unknown to her mate,

One forenoon the she-bird crouch'd not on the nest,
Nor return'd that afternoon, nor the next
Nor ever appear'd again.

And thenceforward all summer in the sound of the sea,
And at night under the full of the moon in calmer weather,
Over the hoarse surging of the sea,
Or flitting from brier to brier by day,
I saw, I heard at intervals the remaining one, the he-bird,
The solitary guest from Alabama.

Blow! Blow! Blow!
Blow up sea-winds along Paumanok's shore;
I wait and I wait till you blow my mate to me.

Yes, when the stars glisten'd,
All night long on the prong of a moss-scallop'd stake,
Down almost amid the slapping waves,
Sat the lone singer wonderful causing tears.

He call'd on his mate,
He pour'd forth the meanings which I of all men know.

Yes my brother I know,
The rest might not, but I have treasur'd every note,
For more than once dimly down to the beach gliding,
Silent, avoiding the moonbeams, blending myself with the
        shadows,
Recalling now the obscure shapes, the echoes, the sounds
        and sights after their sorts,
The white arms out in the breakers tirelessly tossing,
I, with bare feet, a child, the wind wafting my hair,
Listen'd long and long.

Listen'd to keep, to sing, now translating the notes,
Following you my brother.

Soothe ! soothe ! soothe !
Close on its wave soothes the wave behind,
And again another behind embracing and lapping, every one
    close,
But my love soothes not me, not me.

Low hangs the moon, it rose late,
It is lagging — O I think it is heavy with love, with love.

O madly the sea pushes upon the land,
With love, with love.

O night ! do I not see my love fluttering out among the breakers?
What is that little black thing I see there in the white?

Loud ! Loud ! Loud !
Loud I call to you, my love !
High and clear I shoot my voice over the waves,
Surely you must know who is here, is here,
You must know who I am, my love.

Low-hanging moon !
What is that dusky spot in your brown yellow?
O it is the shape, the shape of my mate !
O moon do not keep her from me any longer.

Land ! land ! O land !
Whichever way I turn, O I think you could give me my mate
    back again if you only would,
For I am almost sure I see her dimly whichever way I look.

O rising stars !
Perhaps the one I want so much will rise, will rise with some
    of you..

O throat ! O trembling throat !
Sound clearer through the atmosphere !
Pierce the woods, the earth,
Somewhere listening to catch you must be the one I want.

Shake out carols !
Solitary here, the night's carols !
Carols of lonesome love ! death's carols !
Carols under that lagging, yellow, waning moon !
O under that moon where she droops almost down into the sea !
O reckless despairing carols.

But soft ! sink low !
Soft ! let me just murmur,
And do you wait a moment you husky-nois'd sea,
For somewhere I believe I heard my mate responding to me,
So faint, I must be still, be still to listen,
But not altogether still, for then she might not come immedi-
    ately to me.

Hither my love !
Here I am ! here !
With this just-sustain'd note I announce myself to you,
This gentle call is for you my love, for you.

Do not be decoy'd elsewhere,
That is the whistle of the wind, it is not my voice,
That is the fluttering, the fluttering of the spray,
Those are the shadows of leaves.

O darkness! O in vain!
O I am very sick and sorrowful.

O brown halo in the sky near the moon, drooping upon the sea!
O troubled reflection in the sea!
O throat! O throbbing heart!
And I singing uselessly, uselessly all the night.

O past! O happy life! O songs of joy!
In the air, in the woods, over fields,
Loved! loved! loved! loved! loved!
But my mate no more, no more with me!
We two together no more.

The aria sinking,
All else continuing, the stars shining,
The winds blowing, the notes of the bird continuous echoing,
With angry moans the fierce old mother incessantly moaning,
On the sands of Paumanok's shore gray and rustling,
The yellow half-moon enlarged, sagging down, drooping,
     the face of the sea almost touching,
The boy ecstatic, with his bare feet the waves, with his hair
     the atmosphere dallying,
The love in the heart long pent, now loose, now at last
     tumultuously bursting,
The aria's meaning, the ears, the soul, swiftly depositing,
The strange tears down the cheeks coursing,
The colloquy there, the trio, each uttering,
The undertone, the savage old mother incessantly crying,
To the boy's soul's questions sullenly timing, some drown'd
     secret hissing,
To the outsetting bard.

SONG OF THE UNIVERSAL

1

COME said the Muse,
Sing me a song no poet yet has chanted,
Sing me the universal.

In this broad earth of ours,
Amid the measureless grossness and the slag,
Enclosed and safe within its central heart,
Nestles the seed perfection.

By every life a share or more or less,
None born but it is born, conceal'd or unconceal'd the seed
    is waiting.

2

Lo ! keen-eyed towering science,
As from tall peaks the modern overlooking,
Successive absolute fiats issuing.

Yet again, lo ! the soul, above all science,
For it has history gather'd like husks around the globe,
For it the entire star-myriads roll through the sky.

In spiral routes by long detours,
(As a much-tacking ship upon the sea,)
For it the partial to the permanent flowing,
For it the real to the ideal tends.

For it the mystic evolution,
Not the right only justified, what we call evil also justified.

Forth from their masks, no matter what,
From the huge festering trunk, from craft and guile and
    tears,
Health to emerge and joy, joy universal.

Out of the bulk, the morbid and the shallow,
Out of the bad majority, the varied countless frauds of men
    and states,
Electric, antiseptic yet, cleaving, suffusing all,
Only the good is universal.

3

Over the mountain-growths, disease and sorrow,
An uncaught bird is ever hovering, hovering,
High in the purer, happier air.

From imperfection's murkiest cloud,
Darts always forth one ray of perfect light,
One flash of heaven's glory.

To fashion's, custom's discord,
To the mad Babel-din, the deafening orgies,
Soothing each lull a strain is heard, just heard,
From some far shore the final chorus sounding.

O the blest eyes, the happy hearts,
That see, that know the guiding thread so fine,
Along the mighty labyrinth.

4

And thou America,
For the scheme's culmination, its thought and its reality,
For these (not for thyself) thou hast arrived.

Thou too surroundest all,
Embracing carrying welcoming all, thou too by pathways
    broad and new,
To the ideal tendest.

The measur'd faiths of other lands, the grandeurs of the past,
Are not for thee, but grandeurs of thine own,
Deific faiths and amplitudes, absorbing, comprehending all,
All eligible to all.

All, all for immortality,
Love like the light silently wrapping all,
Nature's amelioration blessing all,
The blossoms, fruits of ages, orchards divine and certain,
Forms, objects, growths, humanities, to spiritual images
    ripening.

Give me O God to sing that thought,
Give me, give him or her I love this quenchless faith,
In Thy ensemble, whatever else withheld withhold not
    from us,
Belief in plan of Thee enclosed in Time and Space,
Health, peace, salvation universal.

Is it a dream?
Nay but the lack of it the dream,
And failing it life's lore and wealth a dream,
And all the world a dream.

PIONEERS! O PIONEERS!

COME my tan-faced children,
Follow well in order, get your weapons ready,
Have you your pistols? have you your sharp-edged axes?
    Pioneers ! O pioneers !

    For we cannot tarry here,
We must march my darlings, we must bear the brunt of
      danger,
We the youthful sinewy races, all the rest on us depend,
    Pioneers ! O pioneers !

    O you youths, Western youths,
So impatient, full of action, full of manly pride and friend-
      ship,
Plain I see you Western youths, see you tramping with the
      foremost,
    Pioneers ! O pioneers !

    Have the elder races halted?
Do they droop and end their lesson, wearied over there
      beyond the seas?
We take up the task eternal, and the burden and the lesson,
    Pioneers ! O pioneers !

All the past we leave behind,
We debouch upon a newer mightier world, varied world,
Fresh and strong the world we seize, world of labor and the
        march,
        Pioneers ! O pioneers !

We detachments steady throwing,
Down the edges, through the passes, up the mountains steep.
Conquering, holding, daring, venturing as we go the un-
        known ways,
        Pioneers ! O pioneers !

We primeval forests felling,
We the rivers stemming, vexing we and piercing deep the
        mines within,
We the surface broad surveying, we the virgin soil up-
        heaving,
        Pioneers ! O pioneers !

Colorado men are we,
From the peaks gigantic, from the great sierras and the
        high plateaus,
From the mine and from the gully, from the hunting trail
        we come,
        Pioneers ! O pioneers !

From Nebraska, from Arkansas,
Central inland race are we, from Missouri, with the con-
        tinental blood intervein'd,
All the hand of comrades clasping, all the Southern, all the
        Northern,
        Pioneers ! O pioneers !

O resistless restless race !
O beloved race in all ! O my breast aches with tender love
      for all !
O I mourn and yet exult, I am rapt with love for all,
      Pioneers ! O pioneers !

      Raise the mighty mother mistress,
Waving high the delicate mistress, over all the starry mis-
      tress, (bend your heads all,)
Raise the fang'd and warlike mistress, stern, impassive,
      weapon'd mistress,
      Pioneers ! O pioneers !

      See my children, resolute children,
By those swarms upon our rear we must never yield or
      falter,
Ages back in ghostly millions frowning there behind us
      urging,
      Pioneers ! O pioneers !

      On and on the compact ranks,
With accessions ever waiting, with the places of the dead
      quickly fill'd,
Through the battle, through defeat, moving yet and never
      stopping,
      Pioneers ! O pioneers !

      O to die advancing on !
Are there some of us to droop and die ? has the hour come ?
Then upon the march we fittest die, soon and sure the gap
      is fill'd,
      Pioneers ! O pioneers !

All the pulses of the world,
Falling in they beat for us, with the Western movement beat,
Holding single or together, steady moving to the front, all
      for us,
    Pioneers ! O pioneers !

    Life's involv'd and varied pageants,
All the forms and shows, all the workmen at their work,
All the seamen and the landsmen, all the masters with their
      slaves,
    Pioneers ! O pioneers !

    All the hapless silent lovers,
All the prisoners in the prisons, all the righteous and the
      wicked,
All the joyous, all the sorrowing, all the living, all the
      dying,
    Pioneers ! O pioneers !

    I too with my soul and body,
We, a curious trio, picking, wandering on our way,
Through these shores amid the shadows, with the appari-
      tions pressing,
    Pioneers ! O pioneers !

    Lo, the darting bowling orb !
Lo, the brother orbs around, all the clustering sons and
      planets,
All the dazzling days, all the mystic nights with dreams,
    Pioneers ! O pioneers !

These are of us, they are with us,
All for primal needed work, while the followers there in
    embryo wait behind,
We to-day's procession heading, we the route for travel
    clearing,
    Pioneers ! O pioneers !

O you daughters of the West !
O you young and elder daughters ! O you mothers and you
    wives !
Never must you be divided, in our ranks you move united,
    Pioneers ! O pioneers !

Minstrels latent on the prairies !
(Shrouded bards of other lands, you may rest, you have
    done your work,)
Soon I hear you coming warbling, soon you rise and tramp
    amid us,
    Pioneers ! O pioneers !

Not for delectations sweet,
Not the cushion and the slipper, not the peaceful and the
    studious,
Not the riches safe and palling, not for us the tame enjoy-
    ment,
    Pioneers ! O pioneers !

Do the feasters gluttonous feast ?
Do the corpulent sleepers sleep ? have they lock'd and
    bolted doors ?
Still be ours the diet hard, and the blanket on the ground,
    Pioneers ! O pioneers !

Has the night descended ?
Was the road of late so toilsome ? did we stop discouraged
    nodding on our way ? *
Yet a passing hour I yield you in your track to pause
    oblivious,
       Pioneers ! O pioneers !

Till with sound of trumpet,
Far, far off the daybreak call—hark ! how loud and clear I
    hear it wind,
Swift ! to the head of the army ! — swift ! spring to your
    places,
       Pioneers ! O pioneers !

DRUM-TAPS

FIRST O SONGS FOR A PRELUDE

FIRST O songs for a prelude,
Lightly strike on the stretch'd tympanum pride and joy in
    my city,
How she led the rest to arms, how she gave the cue,
How at once with lithe limbs unwaiting a moment she
    sprang,
(O superb! O Manhattan, my own, my peerless!
O strongest you in the hour of danger, in crisis! O truer
    than steel!)
How you sprang—how you threw off the costumes of peace
    with indifferent hand,
How your soft opera-music changed, and the drum and fife
    were heard in their stead,
How you led to the war, (that shall serve for our prelude,
    songs of soldiers,)
How Manhattan drum-taps led.

Forty years had I in my city seen soldiers parading,
Forty years as a pageant, till unawares the lady of this
    teeming and turbulent city,
Sleepless amid her ships, her houses, her incalculable
    wealth,
With her million children around her, suddenly,
At dead of night, at news from the south,
Incens'd struck with clinch'd hand the pavement.

A shock electric, the night sustain'd it,
Till with ominous hum our hive at daybreak pour'd out its
    myriads.

From the houses then and the workshops, and through all
    the doorways,
Leapt they tumultuous, and lo! Manhattan arming.

To the drum-taps prompt,
The young men falling in and arming,
The mechanics arming, (the trowel, the jack-plane, the
    blacksmith's hammer, tost aside with precipitation,)
The lawyer leaving his office and arming, the judge leaving
    the court,
The driver deserting his wagon in the street, jumping down,
    throwing the reins abruptly down on the horses' backs,
The salesman leaving the store, the boss, book-keeper,
    porter, all leaving ;
Squads gather everywhere by common consent and arm,
The new recruits, even boys, the old men show them how
    to wear their accoutrements, they buckle the straps
    carefully,
Outdoors arming, indoors arming, the flash of the musket-
    barrels,
The white tents cluster in camps, the arm'd sentries around,
    the sunrise cannon and again at sunset,
Arm'd regiments arrive every day, pass through the city,
    and embark from the wharves,
(How good they look as they tramp down to the river,
    sweaty, with their guns on their shoulders !
How I love them ! how I could hug them, with their brown
    faces and their clothes and knapsacks cover'd with dust !)
The blood of the city up—arm'd ! arm'd ! the cry every-
    where,
The flags flung out from the steeples of churches and from
    all the public buildings and stores,
The tearful parting, the mother kisses her son, the son
    kisses his mother,

(Loth is the mother to part, yet not a word does she speak
    to detain him,)
The tumultuous escort, the ranks of policemen preceding,
    clearing the way,
The unpent enthusiasm, the wild cheers of the crowd for
    their favorites,
The artillery, the silent cannons bright as gold, drawn
    along, rumble lightly over the stones,
(Silent cannons, soon to cease your silence,
Soon unlimber'd to begin the red business;)
All the mutter of preparation, all the determin'd arming,
The hospital service, the lint, bandages and medicines,
The women volunteering for nurses, the work begun for in
    earnest, no mere parade now ;
War ! an arm'd race is advancing ! the welcome for battle,
    no turning away ;
War ! be it weeks, months, or years, an arm'd race is ad-
    vancing to welcome it.

Mannahatta a-march—and it's O to sing it well !
It's O for a manly life in the camp.

And the sturdy artillery,
The guns bright as gold, the work for giants, to serve well
    the guns,
Unlimber them ! (no more as the past forty years for salutes
    for courtesies merely,
Put in something now besides powder and wadding.

And you lady of ships, you Mannahatta,
Old matron of this proud, friendly, turbulent city,
Often in peace and wealth you were pensive or covertly
    frown'd amid all your children,
But now you smile with joy exulting old Mannahatta.

BEAT! BEAT! DRUMS!

BEAT! beat! drums!—blow! bugles! blow!
Through the windows—through doors—burst like a ruthless force,
Into the solemn church, and scatter the congregation,
Into the school where the scholar is studying;
Leave not the bridegroom quiet—no happiness must he
 have now with his bride,
Nor the peaceful farmer any peace, ploughing his field or
 gathering his grain,
So fierce you whirr and pound you drums—so shrill you
 bugles blow.

Beat! beat! drums!—blow! bugles! blow!
Over the traffic of cities—over the rumble of wheels in the
 streets;
Are beds prepared for sleepers at night in the houses? no
 sleepers must sleep in those beds,
No bargainers' bargains by day—no brokers or speculators
 —would they continue?
Would the talkers be talking? would the singer attempt to
 sing?
Would the lawyer rise in the court to state his case before
 the judge?
Then rattle quicker, heavier drums—you bugles wilder
 blow.

Beat ! beat ! drums !—blow ! bugles ! blow !
Make no parley—stop for no expostulation,
Mind not the timid—mind not the weeper or prayer,
Mind not the old man beseeching the young man,
Let not the child's voice be heard, nor the mother's en-
    treaties,
Make even the trestles to shake the dead where they lie
    awaiting the hearses,
So strong you thump O terrible drums—so loud you bugles
    blow.

CAVALRY CROSSING A FORD

A LINE in long array where they wind betwixt green islands,
They take a serpentine course, their arms flash in the sun
    —hark to the musical clank,
Behold the silvery river, in it the splashing horses loiter-
    ing stop to drink,
Behold the brown-faced men, each group, each person, a
    picture, the negligent rest on the saddles,
Some emerge on the opposite bank, others are just enter-
    ing the ford—while,
Scarlet and blue and snowy white,
The guidon flags flutter gayly in the wind.

BY THE BIVOUAC'S FITFUL FLAME

By the bivouac's fitful flame,
A procession winding around me, solemn and sweet and
    slow—but first I note,
The tents of the sleeping army, the fields' and woods' dim
    outline,
The darkness lit by spots of kindled fire, the silence,
Like a phantom far or near an occasional figure moving,
The shrubs and trees, (as I lift my eyes they seem to be
    stealthily watching me,)
While wind in procession thoughts, O tender and wondrous
    thoughts,
Of life and death, of home and the past and loved, and of
    those that are far away;
A solemn and slow procession there as I sit on the ground,
By the bivouac's fitful flame.

COME UP FROM THE FIELDS FATHER

COME up from the fields father, here's a letter from our
     Pete,
And come to the front door mother, here's a letter from
     thy dear son.

Lo, 'tis autumn,
Lo, where the trees, deeper green, yellower and redder,
Cool and sweeten Ohio's villages with leaves fluttering in
     the moderate wind,
Where apples ripe in the orchards hang and grapes on the
     trellis'd vines,
(Smell you the smell of the grapes on the vines?
Smell you the buckweat where the bees were lately buzz-
     ing?)

Above all, lo, the sky so calm, so transparent after the
     rain, and with wondrous clouds,
Below too, all calm, all vital and beautiful, and the farm
     prospers well.

Down in the fields all prospers well,
But now from the fields come father, come at the daugh-
     ter's call,
And come to the entry mother, to the front door come
     right away.

Fast as she can she hurries, something ominous, her steps
     trembling,
She does not tarry to smooth her hair nor adjust her cap.

Open the envelope quickly,
O this is not our son's writing, yet his name is sign'd,
O a strange hand writes for our dear son, O stricken
     mother's soul !
All swims before her eyes, flashes with black, she catches
     the main words only,
Sentences broken, *gunshot wound in the breast, cavalry
     skirmish, taken to hospital,*
At present low, but will soon be better.

Ah now the single figure to me,
Amid all teeming and wealthy Ohio with all its cities and farms,
Sickly white in the face and dull in the head, very faint,
By the jamb of a door leans.

Grieve not so, dear mother, (the just-grown daughter speaks
     through her sobs,
The little sisters huddle around speechless and dismay'd,)
See, dearest mother, the letter says Pete will soon be better.

Alas poor boy, he will never be better, (nor may-be needs
     to be better, that brave and simple soul,)
While they stand at home at the door he is dead already,
The only son is dead.

But the mother needs to be better,
She with thin form presently drest in black,
By day her meals untouch'd, then at night fitfully sleeping,
     often waking,
In the midnight waking, weeping, longing with one deep
     longing,
O that she might withdraw unnoticed, silent from life
     escape and withdraw,
To follow, to seek, to be with her dear dead son.

THE WOUND-DRESSER

1

An old man bending I come among new faces,
Years looking backward resuming in answer to children,
Come tell us old man, as from young men and maidens
    that love me,
(Arous'd and angry, I'd thought to beat the alarum, and
    urge relentless war,
But soon my fingers fail'd me, my face droop'd and I re-
    sign'd myself,
To sit by the wounded and soothe them, or silently watch
    the dead;)
Years hence of these scenes, of these furious passions,
    these chances,
Of unsurpass'd heroes, (was one side so brave? the other
    was equally brave;)
Now be witness again, paint the mightiest armies of earth,
Of those armies so rapid so wondrous what saw you to
    tell us?
What stays with you latest and deepest? of curious panics,
Of hard-fought engagements or sieges tremendous what
    deepest remains?

2

O maidens and young men I love and that love me,
What you ask of my days those the strangest and sudden
    your talking recalls,

Soldier alert I arrive after a long march cover'd with sweat
    and dust,
In the nick of time I come, plunge in the fight, loudly
    shout in the rush of successful charge,
Enter the captur'd works—yet lo, like a swift-running
    river they fade,
Pass and are gone they fade—I dwell not on soldiers'
    perils or soldiers' joys,
(Both I remember well—many the hardships, few the joys,
    yet I was content.)

But in silence, in dreams' projections,
While the world of gain and appearance and mirth goes on,
So soon what is over forgotten, and waves wash the im-
    prints off the sand,
With hinged knees returning I enter the doors, (while for
    you up there,
Whoever you are, follow without noise and be of strong
    heart.)

Bearing the bandages, water and sponge,
Straight and swift to my wounded I go,
Where they lie on the ground after the battle brought in,
Where their priceless blood reddens the grass the ground,
Or to the rows of the hospital tent, or under the roof'd
    hospital,
To the long rows of cots up and down each side I return,
To each and all one after another I draw near, not one do
    I miss,
An attendant follows holding a tray, he carries a refuse
    pail,
Soon to be fill'd with clotted rags and blood, emptied, and
    fill'd again.

I onward go, I stop,
With hinged knees and steady hand to dress wounds,
I am firm with each, the pangs are sharp yet unavoidable,
One turns to me his appealing eyes—poor boy ! I never
    knew you,
Yet I think I could not refuse this moment to die for you,
    if that would save you.

3

On, on I go, (open doors of time. open hospital doors!)
The crush'd head I dress, (poor crazed hand tear not the
    bandage away,)
The neck of the cavalry-man with the bullet through and
    through I examine,
Hard the breathing rattles, quite glazed already the eye,
    yet life struggles hard,
(Come sweet death! be persuaded O beautiful death!
In mercy come quickly.)

From the stump of the arm, the amputated hand,
I undo the clotted lint, remove the slough, wash off the
    matter and blood,
Back on his pillow the soldier bends with curv'd neck and
    side-falling head,
His eyes are closed, his face is pale, he dares not look on
    the bloody stump,
And has not yet look'd on it.

I dress a wound in the side, deep, deep,
But a day or two more, for see the frame all wasted and
    sinking,
And the yellow-blue countenance see.

I dress the perforated shoulder, the foot with the bullet-
     wound,
Cleanse the one with a gnawing and putrid gangrene, so
     sickening, so offensive,
While the attendant stands behind aside me holding the
     tray and pail.

I am faithful, I do not give out,
The fractur'd thigh, the knee, the wound in the abdomen,
These and more I dress with impassive hand, (yet deep in
     my breast a fire, a burning flame.)

4

Thus in silence in dreams' projections,
Returning, resuming, I tread my way through the hos-
     pitals,
The hurt and wounded I pacify with soothing hand,
I sit by the restless all the dark night, some are so young,
Some suffer so much, I recall the experience sweet and sad,
(Many a soldier's loving arms about this neck have cross'd
     and rested,
Many a soldier's kiss dwells on these bearded lips.)

ETHIOPIA SALUTING THE COLORS

WHO are you dusky woman, so ancient hardly human,
With your woolly-white and turban'd head, and bare bony
    feet?
Why rising by the roadside here, do you the colors greet?

('Tis while our army lines Carolina's sand and pines,
Forth from thy hovel door thou Ethiopia com'st to me,
As under doughty Sherman I march toward the sea.)

Me master years a hundred since from my parents sunder'd,
A little child, they caught me as the savage beast is caught,
Then hither me across the sea the cruel slaver brought.

No further does she say, but lingering all the day,
Her high-borne turban'd head she wags, and rolls her
    darkling eye,
And courtesies to the regiments, the guidons moving by.

What is it fateful woman, so blear, hardly human?
Why wag your head with turban bound, yellow, red and
    green?
Are the things so strange and marvelous you see or have
    seen?

TO A CERTAIN CIVILIAN

Did you ask dulcet rhymes from me?
Did you seek the civilian's peaceful and languishing
     rhymes?
Did you find what I sang erewhile so hard to follow?
Why I was not singing erewhile for you to follow, to
     understand—nor am I now;
(I have been born of the same as the war was born,
The drum-corps' rattle is ever to me sweet music, I love
     well the martial dirge,
With slow wail and convulsive throb leading the officer's
     funeral;)
What to such as you anyhow such a poet as I? therefore
     leave my works,
And go lull yourself with what you can understand, and
     with piano-tunes,
For I lull nobody, and you will never understand me.

SPIRIT WHOSE WORK IS DONE

(Washington City, 1865)

Spirit whose work is done—spirit of dreadful hours!
Ere departing fade from my eyes your forests of bayonets;
Spirit of gloomiest fears and doubts, (yet onward ever un-
      faltering pressing,)
Spirit of many a solemn day and many a savage scene—
      electric spirit,
That with muttering voice through the war now closed,
      like a tireless phantom flitted,
Rousing the land with breath of flame, while you beat and
      beat the drum,
Now as the sound of the drum, hollow and harsh to the
      last, reverberates round me,
As your ranks, your immortal ranks, return, return from
      the battles,
As the muskets of the young men yet lean over their
      shoulders,
As I look on the bayonets bristling over their shoulders,
As those slanted bayonets, whole forests of them appearing
      in the distance, approach and pass on, returning home-
      ward,
Moving with steady motion, swaying to and fro to the right
      and left,
Evenly lightly rising and falling while the steps keep time;
Spirit of hours I knew, all hectic red one day, but pale as
      death next day,

Touch my mouth ere you depart, press my lips close,
Leave me your pulses of rage—bequeath them to me—fill
    me with currents convulsive,
Let them scorch and blister out of my chants when you are
    gone,
Let them identify you to the future in these songs.

MEMORIES OF PRESIDENT LINCOLN

WHEN LILACS LAST IN THE DOORYARD
BLOOM'D

1

WHEN lilacs last in the dooryard bloom'd,
And the great star early droop'd in the western sky in the
    night,
I mourn'd, and yet shall mourn with ever-returning spring.

Ever-returning spring, trinity sure to me you bring,
Lilac blooming perennial and drooping star in the west,
And thought of him I love.

2

O powerful western fallen star!
O shades of night—O moody, tearful night!
O great star disappear'd—O the black murk that hides the
    star!
O cruel hands that hold me powerless—O helpless soul of
    me!
O harsh surrounding cloud that will not free my soul.

3

In the dooryard fronting an old farm-house near the white-
    wash'd palings,
Stands the lilac-bush tall-growing with heart-shaped leaves
    of rich green,

With many a pointed blossom rising delicate, with the per
    fume strong I love,
With every leaf a miracle—and from this bush in the door-
    yard,
With delicate-color'd blossoms and heart-shaped leaves of
    rich green,
A sprig with its flower I break.

4

In the swamp in secluded recesses,
A shy and hidden bird is warbling a song.

Solitary the thrush,
The hermit withdrawn to himself, avoiding the settlements,
Sings by himself a song.

Song of the bleeding throat,
Death's outlet song of life, (for well dear brother I know,
If thou wast not granted to sing thou would'st surely die.)

5

Over the breast of the spring, the land, amid cities,
Amid lanes and through old woods, where lately the vio-
    lets peep'd from the ground, spotting the gray debris,
Amid the grass in the fields each side of the lanes, passing
    the endless grass,
Passing the yellow-spear'd wheat, every grain from its
    shroud in the dark-brown fields uprisen,
Passing the apple-tree blows of white and pink in the or-
    chards,
Carrying a corpse to where it shall rest in the grave,
Night and day journeys a coffin.

6

Coffin that passes through lanes and streets
Through day and night with the great cloud darkening the
    land,
With the pomp of the inloop'd flags with the cities draped
    in black,
With the show of the States themselves as of crape-veil'd
    women standing,
With processions long and winding and the flambeaus of
    the night,
With the countless torches lit, with the silent sea of faces
    and the unbared heads,
With the waiting depot, the arriving coffin, and the sombre
    faces,
With dirges through the night, with the thousand voices
    rising strong and solemn,
With all the mournful voices of the dirges pour'd around
    the coffin,
The dim-lit churches and the shuddering organs—where
    amid these you journey,
With the tolling tolling bells' perpetual clang,
Here, coffin that slowly passes,
I give you my sprig of lilac.

7

(Nor for you, for one alone,
Blossoms and branches green to coffins all I bring,
For fresh as the morning, thus would I chant a song for
    you O sane and sacred death.

All over bouquets of roses,
O death, I cover you over with roses and early lilies,

But mostly and now the lilac that blooms the first,
Copious I break, I break the sprigs from the bushes,
With loaded arms I come, pouring for you,
For you and the coffins all of you O death.)

8

O western orb sailing the heaven,
Now I know what you must have meant as a month since I
    walk'd,
As I walk'd in silence the transparent shadowy night,
As I saw you had something to tell as you bent to me
    night after night,
As you droop'd from the sky low down as if to my side,
    (while the other stars all look'd on,)
As we wander'd together the solemn night, (for something
    I know not what kept me from sleep,)
As the night advanced, and I saw on the rim of the west
    how full you were of woe,
As I stood on the rising ground in the breeze in the cool
    transparent night,
As I watch'd where you pass'd and was lost in the nether-
    ward black of the night,
As my soul in its trouble dissatisfied sank, as where you
    sad orb,
Concluded, dropt in the night, and was gone.

9

Sing on there in the swamp,
O singer bashful and tender, I hear your notes, I hear your
    call,

I hear, I come presently, I understand you,
But a moment I linger, for the lustrous star has detain'd
    me,
The star my departing comrade holds and detains me.

10

O how shall I warble myself for the dead one there I loved ?
And how shall I deck my song for the large sweet soul that
    has gone ?
And what shall my perfume be for the grave of him I love ?

Sea-winds blow, from east and west
Blown from the Eastern sea and blown from the Western
    sea, till there on the prairies meeting,
These and with these and the breath of my chant,
I'll perfume the grave of him I love.

11

O what shall I hang on the chamber walls ?
And what shall the pictures be that I hang on the walls,
To adorn the burial-house of him I love ?

Pictures of growing spring and farms and homes,
With the Fourth-month eve at sundown, and the gray smoke
    lucid and bright,
With floods of the yellow gold of the gorgeous, indolent,
    sinking sun, burning, expanding the air,
With the fresh sweet herbage under foot, and the pale
    green leaves of the trees prolific,
In the distance the flowing glaze, the breast of the river,
    with a wind-dapple here and there,
With ranging hills on the banks, and many a line against
    the sky, and shadows,

And the city at hand with dwellings so dense, and stacks of
     chimneys,
And all the scenes of life and the workshops, and the work-
     men homeward returning.

12

Lo, body and soul—this land,
My own Manhattan with spires, and the sparkling and
     hurrying tides, and the ships,
The varied and ample land, the South and the North in the
     light, Ohio's shores and flashing Missouri,
And ever the far-spreading prairies cover'd with grass and
     corn.

Lo, the most excellent sun so calm and haughty,
The violet and purple morn with just-felt breezes,
The gentle soft-born measureless light,
The miracle spreading bathing all, the fulfill'd noon,
The coming eve delicious, the welcome night and the stars,
Over my cities shining all, enveloping man and land.

13

Sing on, sing on you gray-brown bird,
Sing from the swamps, the recesses, pour your chant from
     the bushes,
Limitless out of the dusk, out of the cedars and pines.

Sing on dearest brother, warble your reedy song,
Loud human song, with voice of uttermost woe.

O liquid and free and tender!
O wild and loose to my soul—O wondrous singer!

You only I hear—yet the star holds me, (but will soon de-
    part,)
Yet the lilac with mastering odor holds me.

14

Now while I sat in the day and look'd forth,
In the close of the day with its light and the fields of spring,
    and the farmers preparing their crops,
In the large unconscious scenery of my land with its lakes
    and forests,
In the heavenly aerial beauty, (after the perturb'd winds
    and the storms,)
Under the arching heavens of the afternoon swift passing,
    and the voices of children and women,
The many-moving sea-tides, and I saw the ships how they
    sail'd,
And the summer approaching with richness, and the fields
    all busy with labor,
And the infinite separate houses, how they all went on, each
    with its meals and minutia of daily usages,
And the streets how their throbbings throbb'd, and the
    cities pent—lo, then and there,
Falling upon them all and among them all, enveloping me
    with the rest,
Appear'd the cloud, appear'd the long black trail,
And I knew death, its thought, and the sacred knowledge of
    death.

Then with the knowledge of death as walking one side of
    me,
And the thought of death close-walking the other side of me,
And I in the middle as with companions, and as holding the
    hands of companions,

I fled forth to the hiding receiving night that talks not,
Down to the shores of the water, the path by the swamp in
    the dimness,
To the solemn shadowy cedars and ghostly pines so still.

And the singer so shy to the rest receiv'd me,
The gray-brown bird I know receiv'd us comrades three,
And he sang the carol of death, and a verse for him I love.

From deep secluded recesses,
From the fragrant cedars and the ghostly pines so still,
Came the carol of the bird.

And the charm of the carol rapt me,
As I held as if by their hands my comrades in the night,
And the voice of my spirit tallied the song of the bird.

Come lovely and soothing death,
Undulate round the world, serenely arriving, arriving,
In the day, in the night, to all, to each,
Sooner or later delicate death.

Prais'd be the fathomless universe,
For life and joy, and for objects and knowledge curious,
And for love, sweet love—but praise! praise! praise!
For the sure-enwinding arms of cool-enfolding death.

Dark mother always gliding near with soft feet,
Have none chanted for thee a chant of fullest welcome?
Then I chant it for thee, I glorify thee above all,
I bring thee a song that when thou must indeed come, come un-
    falteringly.

Approach strong deliveress,
When it is so, when thou hast taken them I joyously sing the
    dead,
Lost in the loving floating ocean of thee,
Laved in the flood of thy bliss O death.

From me to thee glad serenades,
Dances for thee I propose saluting thee, adornments and feast-
    ings for thee,
And the sights of the open landscape and the high-spread sky
    are fitting,
And life and the fields, and the huge and thoughtful night.

The night in silence under many a star,
The ocean shore and the husky whispering wave whose voice I
    know,
And the soul turning to thee O vast and well-veil'd death,
And the body gratefully nestling close to thee.

Over the tree-tops I float thee a song,
Over the rising and sinking waves, over the myriad fields and
    the prairies wide,
Over the dense-pack'd cities all and the teeming wharves and
    ways,
I float this carol with joy, with joy to thee O death.

15

To the tally of my soul,
Loud and strong kept up the gray-brown bird,
With pure deliberate notes spreading filling the night.

Loud in the pines and cedars dim,
Clear in the freshness moist and the swamp-perfume,
And I with my comrades there in the night.

While my sight that was bound in my eyes unclosed,
As to long panoramas of visions.

And I saw askant the armies,
I saw as in noiseless dreams hundreds of battle-flags,
Borne through the smoke of the battles and pierc'd with
    missiles I saw them,
And carried hither and yon through the smoke, and torn
    and bloody,
And at last but a few shreds left on the staffs, (and all in
    silence,)
And the staffs all splinter'd and broken.

I saw battle-corpses, myriads of them,
And the white skeletons of young men, I saw them,
I saw the debris and debris of all the slain soldiers of the
    war,
But I saw they were not as was thought,
They themselves were fully at rest, they suffer'd not,
The living remain'd and suffer'd, the mother suffer'd,
And the wife and the child and the musing comrade suffer'd,
And the armies that remain'd suffer'd.

16

Passing the visions, passing the night,
Passing, unloosing the hold of my comrades' hands,
Passing the song of the hermit bird and the tallying song
    of my soul,
Victorious song, death's outlet song, yet varying ever-
    altering song,
As low and wailing, yet clear the notes, rising and falling,
    flooding the night,

Sadly sinking and fainting, as warning and warning, and
    yet again bursting with joy,
Covering the earth and filling the spread of heaven,
As that powerful psalm in the night I heard from recesses,
Passing, I leave thee lilac with heart-shaped leaves,
I leave thee there in the door-yard, blooming, returning
    with spring.

I cease from my song for thee,
From my gaze on thee in the west, fronting the west, com-
    muning with thee,
O comrade lustrous with silver face in the night.

Yet each to keep and all, retrievements out of the night,
The song, the wondrous chant of the gray-brown bird,
And the tallying chant, the echo arous'd in my soul,
With the lustrous and drooping star with the countenance
    full of woe,
With the holders holding my hand nearing the call of the
    bird,
Comrades mine and I in the midst, and their memory ever
    to keep, for the dead I loved so well,
For the sweetest, wisest soul of all my days and lands—and
    this for his dear sake,
Lilac and star and bird twined with the chant of my soul,
There in the fragrant pines and the cedars dusk and dim.

O CAPTAIN! MY CAPTAIN!

O CAPTAIN! my Captain! our fearful trip is done,
The ship has weather'd every rack, the prize we sought is
      won,
The port is near, the bells I hear, the people all exulting,
While follow eyes the steady keel, the vessel grim and daring;
          But O heart! heart! heart!
          O the bleeding drops of red,
              Where on the deck my Captain lies,
                  Fallen cold and dead.

O Captain! my Captain! rise up and hear the bells;
Rise up—for you the flag is flung—for you the bugle trills,
For you bouquets and ribbon'd wreaths—for you the shores
      a-crowding,
For you they call, the swaying mass, their eager faces
      turning;
          Here Captain! dear father!
          This arm beneath your head!
              It is some dream that on the deck,
                  You've fallen cold and dead.

My Captain does not answer, his lips are pale and still,
My father does not feel my arm, he has no pulse nor will,
The ship is anchor'd safe and sound, its voyage closed and
      done,
From fearful trip the victor ship comes in with object won;
          Exult O shores, and ring O bells!
          But I with mournful tread,
              Walk the deck my Captain lies,
                  Fallen cold and dead.

HUSH'D BE THE CAMPS TO-DAY

(May 4, 1865)

HUSH'D be the camps to-day,
And soldiers let us drape our war-worn weapons,
And each with musing soul retire to celebrate,
Our dear commander's death.

No more for him life's stormy conflicts,
Nor victory, nor defeat—no more time's dark events,
Charging like ceaseless clouds across the sky.

But sing poet in our name,
Sing of the love we bore him—because you, dweller in
    camps, know it truly.

As they invault the coffin there,
Sing—as they close the doors of earth upon him—one verse,
For the heavy hearts of soldiers.

OLD AGE, DEATH, AND IMMORTALITY

OF THAT BLITHE THROAT OF THINE *

OF that blithe throat of thine from arctic bleak and blank,
I'll mind the lesson, solitary bird—let me too welcome
    chilling drifts,
E'en the profoundest chill, as now—a torpid pulse, a brain
    unnerv'd,
Old age land-lock'd within its winter bay—(cold, cold, O
    cold!)
These snowy hairs, my feeble arm, my frozen feet,
For them thy faith, thy rule I take, and grave it to the last;
Not summer's zones alone—not chants of youth, or south's
    warm tides alone,
But held by sluggish floes, pack'd in the northern ice, the
    cumulus of years,
These with gay heart I also sing.

*More than eighty-three degrees north—about a good day's steaming dis-
tance to the Pole by one of our fast oceaners in clear water—Greely the ex-
plorer heard the song of a single snow-bird merrily sounding over the desolation.

THANKS IN OLD AGE

THANKS in old age—thanks ere I go,
For health, the midday sun, the impalpable air—for life,
    mere life,
For precious ever-lingering memories, (of you my mother
    dear—you, father—you, brothers, sisters, friends,)
For all my days—not those of peace alone—the days of war
    the same,
For gentle words, caresses, gifts from foreign lands,
For shelter, wine and meat—for sweet appreciation,
(You distant, dim unknown—or young or old—countless,
    unspecified, readers belov'd,
We never met, and ne'er shall meet—and yet our souls em-
    brace, long, close and long;)
For beings, groups, love, deeds, words, books—for colors,
    forms,
For all the brave strong men—devoted, hardy men—who've
    forward sprung in freedom's help, all years, all lands,
For braver, stronger, more devoted men—(a special laurel
    ere I go, to life's war's chosen ones,
The cannoneers of song and thought—the great artillerists
    —the foremost leaders, captains of the soul:)
As soldier from an ended war return'd—As traveler out of
    myriads, to the long procession retrospective,
Thanks—joyful thanks!—a soldier's, traveler's thanks.

ON, ON THE SAME, YE JOCUND TWAIN!

ON, on the same, ye jocund twain!
My life and recitative, containing birth, youth, mid-age
   years,
Fitful as motley-tongues of flame, inseparably twined and
   merged in one—combining all,
My single soul—aims, confirmations, failures, joys—Nor
   single soul alone,
I chant my nation's crucial stage, (America's, haply humanity's)—the trial great, the victory great,
A strange *eclaircissement* of all the masses past, the eastern
   world, the ancient, medieval,
Here, here from wanderings, strayings, lessons, wars, defeats—here at the west a voice triumphant—justifying
   all,
A gladsome pealing cry—a song for once of utmost pride
   and satisfaction;
I chant from it the common bulk, the general average horde,
   (the best no sooner than the worst)—And now I chant
   old age,
(My verses, written first for forenoon life, and for the
   summer's, autumn's spread,
I pass to snow-white hairs the same, and give to pulses
   winter-cool'd the same;)
As here in careless trill, I and my recitatives, with faith
   and love,
Wafting to other work, to unknown songs, conditions,
On, on, ye jocund twain! continue on the same!

OLD AGE'S LAMBENT PEAKS

THE touch of flame—the illuminating fire—the loftiest look
    at last,
O'er city, passion, sea—o'er prairie, mountain, wood—the
    earth itself;
The airy, different, changing hues of all, in falling twi-
    light,
Objects and groups, bearings, faces, reminiscences;
The calmer sight—the golden setting, clear and broad:
So much i' the atmosphere, the points of view, the situ-
    ations whence we scan,
Bro't out by them alone—so much (perhaps the best) un-
    reck'd before;
The lights indeed from them—old age's lambent peaks.

TO GET THE FINAL LILT OF SONGS

To get the final lilt of songs,
To penetrate the inmost lore of poets—to know the mighty
    ones,
Job, Homer, Eschylus, Dante, Shakspere, Tennyson, Em-
    erson;
To diagnose the shifting-delicate tints of love and pride and
    doubt—to truly understand,
To encompass these, the last keen faculty and entrance-
    price,
Old age, and what it brings from all its past experiences.

HALCYON DAYS

Not from successful love alone,
Not wealth, nor honor'd middle age, nor victories of politics or war;
But as life wanes, and all the turbulent passions calm,
As gorgeous, vapory, silent hues cover the evening sky,
As softness, fulness, rest, suffuse the frame, like fresher, balmier air,
As the days take on a mellower light, and the apple at last hangs really finish'd and indolent-ripe on the tree,
Then for the teeming quietest, happiest days of all !
The brooding and blissful halcyon days !

OLD AGE'S SHIP & CRAFTY DEATH'S

FROM east and west across the horizon's edge,
Two mighty masterful vessels sailers steal upon us:
But we'll make race a-time upon the seas—a battle-contest
    yet ! bear lively there !
(Our joys of strife and derring-do to the last !)
Put on the old ship all her power to-day !
Crowd top-sail, top-gallant and royal studding-sails,
Out challenge and defiance—flags and flaunting pennants
    added,
As we take to the open—take to the deepest, freest waters.

AFTER THE SUPPER·AND TALK

AFTER the supper and talk—after the day is done,
As a friend from friends his final withdrawal prolonging,
Good-bye and Good-bye with emotional lips repeating,
(So hard for his hand to release those hands—no more
    will they meet,
No more for communion of sorrow and joy, of old and
    young,
A far-stretching journey awaits him, to return no more,)
Shunning, postponing severance—seeking to ward off the
    last word ever so little,
E'en at the exit-door turning—charges superfluous calling
    back—e'en as he descends the steps,
Something to eke out a minute additional—shadows of
    nightfall deepening,
Farewells, messages lessening—dimmer the forthgoer's
    visage and form,
Soon to be lost for aye in the darkness—loth, O so loth to
    depart !
Garrulous to the very last.

WHISPERS OF HEAVENLY DEATH

WHISPERS of heavenly death murmur'd I hear,
Labial gossip of night, sibilant chorals,
Footsteps gently ascending, mystical breezes wafted soft
    and low,
Ripples of unseen rivers, tides of a current flowing, forever
    flowing,
(Or is it the plashing of tears? the measureless waters of
    human tears?)

I see, just see skyward, great cloud-masses,
Mournfully slowly they roll, silently swelling and mixing,
With at times a half-dimm'd sadden'd far-off star,
Appearing and disappearing.

(Some parturition rather, some solemn immortal birth;
On the frontiers to eyes impenetrable,
Some soul is passing over.)

·

JOY, SHIPMATE, JOY !

Joy, shipmate, joy !
(Pleas'd to my soul at death I cry,)
Our life is closed, our life begins,
The long, long anchorage we leave,
The ship is clear at last, she leaps !
She swiftly courses from the shore,
Joy, shipmate, joy.

LEAVES OF GRASS

Come, said my Soul,
Such verses for my Body let us write, (for we are one,)
That should I after death invisibly return,
Or, long, long hence, in other spheres,
There to some group of mates the chants resuming,
(Tallying Earth's soil, trees, winds, tumultuous waves,)
Ever with pleas'd smile I may keep on,
Ever and ever yet the verses owning—as, first, I here and now,
Signing for Soul and Body, set to them my name,

Walt Whitman

INSCRIPTIONS

ONE'S-SELF I SING

ONE'S-SELF I sing, a simple separate person,
Yet utter the word Democratic, the word En-Masse.

Of physiology from top to toe I sing,
Not physiognomy alone nor brain alone is worthy for the
    Muse, I say the Form complete is worthier far,
The Female equally with the Male I sing.

Of Life immense in passion, pulse, and power,
Cheerful, for freest action form'd under the laws divine,
The Modern Man I sing.

TO FOREIGN LANDS

I HEARD that you ask'd for something to prove this puzzle
    the New World,
And to define America, her athletic Democracy,
Therefore I send you my poems that you behold in them
    what you wanted.

I HEAR AMERICA SINGING

I HEAR America singing, the varied carols I hear,
Those of mechanics, each one singing his as it should be
    blithe and strong,
The carpenter singing his as he measures his plank or
    beam,
The mason singing as he makes ready for work, or leaves
    off work,

The boatman singing what belongs to him in his boat, the
     deck-hand singing on the steamboat deck,
The shoemaker singing as he sits on his bench, the hatter
     singing as he stands,
The wood-cutter's song, the ploughboy's on his way in the
     morning, or at noon intermission or at sundown,
The delicious singing of the mother, or of the young wife
     at work, or of the girl sewing or washing,
Each singing what belongs to him or her and to none else,
The day what belongs to the day—at night the party of
     young fellows, robust, friendly,
Singing with open mouths their strong melodious songs.

SHUT NOT YOUR DOORS

SHUT not your doors to me proud libraries,
For that which was lacking on all your well-fill'd shelves,
     yet needed most, I bring,
Forth from the war emerging, a book I have made,
The words of my book nothing, the drift of it every thing,
A book separate, not link'd with the rest nor felt by the
     intellect,
But you ye untold latencies will thrill to every page.

STARTING FROM PAUMANOK

STARTING from fish-shape Paumanok where I was born,
Well-begotten, and rais'd by a perfect mother,
After roaming many lands, lover of populous pavements,
Dweller in Mannahatta my city, or on southern savannas,
Or a soldier camp'd or carrying my knapsack and gun, or a
    miner in California,
Or rude in my home in Dakota's woods, my diet meat, my
    drink from the spring,
Or withdrawn to muse and meditate in some deep recess,
Far from the clank of crowds intervals passing rapt and
    happy,
Aware of the fresh free giver the flowing Missouri, aware
    of mighty Niagara,
Aware of the buffalo herds grazing the plains, the hirsute
    and strong-breasted bull,
Of earth, rocks, Fifth-month flowers experienced, stars,
    rain, snow, my amaze,
Having studied the mocking-bird's tones and the flight of
    the mountain-hawk,
And heard at dusk the unrivall'd one, the hermit thrush
    from the swamp-cedars,
Solitary, singing in the West, I strike up for a New World.

SONG OF MYSELF

1

I CELEBRATE myself, and sing myself,
And what I assume you shall assume,
For every atom belonging to me as good belongs to you.

I loafe and invite my soul,
I lean and loafe at my ease observing a spear of summer
    grass.

My tongue, every atom of my blood, form'd from this soil,
    this air,
Born here of parents born here from parents the same, and
    their parents the same,
I, now thirty-seven years old in perfect health begin,
Hoping to cease not till death.

Creeds and schools in abeyance,
Retiring back a while sufficed at what they are, but never
    forgotten,
I harbor for good or bad, I permit to speak at every hazard,
Nature without check with original energy.

.   .   .   .   .

2

Have you reckon'd a thousand acres much? have you reck-
    on'd the earth much?
Have you practis'd so long to learn to read?
Have you felt so proud to get at the meaning of poems?

Stop this day and night with me and you shall possess the
    origin of all poems,
You shall possess the good of the earth and sun, (there are
    millions of suns left,)
You shall no longer take things at second or third hand, nor
    look through the eyes of the dead, nor feed on the
    spectres in books,
You shall not look through my eyes either, nor take things
    from me,
You shall listen to all sides and filter them from your self.

     ·   ·   ·   ·   ·

6

A child said *What is the grass?* fetching it to me with full
    hands;
How could I answer the child? I do not know what it is
    any more than he.

I guess it must be the flag of my disposition, out of hope-
    ful green stuff woven.

Or I guess it is the handkerchief of the Lord,
A scented gift and remembrancer designedly dropt,
Bearing the owner's name someway in the corners, that
    we may see and remark, and say *Whose?*

Or I guess the grass is itself a child, the produced babe of
    the vegetation.

Or I guess it is a uniform hieroglyphic,
And it means, Sprouting alike in broad zones and narrow
    zones,

Growing among black folks as among white,
Kanuck, Tuckahoe, Congressman, Cuff, I give them the
    same, I receive them the same.

And now it seems to me the beautiful uncut hair of graves.

Tenderly will I use you curling grass,
It may be you transpire from the breasts of young men,
It may be if I had known them I would have loved them,
It may be you are from old people, or from offspring taken
    soon out of their mothers' laps,
And here you are the mothers' laps.

This grass is very dark to be from the white heads of old
    mothers,
Darker than the colorless beards of old men,
Dark to come from under the faint red roofs of mouths.

O I perceive after all so many uttering tongues,
And I perceive they do not come from the roofs of mouths
    for nothing.

I wish I could translate the hints about the dead young men
    and women,
And the hints about old men and mothers, and the offspring
    taken soon out of their laps.

What do you think has become of the young and old men?
And what do you think has become of the women and chil-
    dren?

They are alive and well somewhere,
The smallest sprout shows there is really no death,
And if ever there was it led forward life, and does not wait
    at the end to arrest it,
And ceas'd the moment life appear'd.

All goes onward and outward, nothing collapses,
And to die is different from what any one supposed, and
    luckier.

     .   .   .   .   .

10

Alone far in the wilds and mountains I hunt,
Wandering amazed at my own lightness and glee,
In the late afternoon choosing a safe spot to pass the night,
Kindling a fire and broiling the fresh-kill'd game,
Falling asleep on the gather'd leaves with my dog and gun
    by my side.

The Yankee clipper is under her sky-sails, she cuts the
    sparkle and scud,
My eyes settle the land, I bend at her prow or shout joy-
    ously from the deck.

The boatmen and clam-diggers arose early and stopt for me,
I tuck'd my trowser-ends in my boots and went and had a
    good time;
You should have been with us that day round the chowder-
    kettle.

I saw the marriage of the trapper in the open air in the far
    west, the bride was a red girl,
Her father and his friends sat near cross-legged and dumbly
    smoking, they had moccasins to their feet and large
    thick blankets hanging from their shoulders,
On a bank lounged the trapper, he was drest mostly in
    skins, his luxuriant beard and curls protected his neck,
    he held his bride by the hand,
She had long eyelashes, her head was bare, her coarse
    straight locks descended upon her voluptuous limbs
    and reach'd to her feet.

The runaway slave came to my house and stopt outside,
I heard his motions crackling the twigs of the woodpile,
Through the swung half-door of the kitchen I saw him
    limpsy and weak,
And went where he sat on a log and led him in and assured
    him,
And brought water and fill'd a tub for his sweated body
    and bruis'd feet,
And gave him a room that enter'd from my own, and gave
    him some coarse clean clothes,
And remember perfectly well his revolving eyes and his
    awkwardness,
And remember putting plasters on the galls of his neck and
    ankles;
He staid with me a week before he was recuperated and
    pass'd north,
I had him sit next me at table, my fire-lock lean'd in the
    corner.

.   .   .   .   .

13

The negro holds firmly the reins of his four horses, the
    block swags underneath on its tied-over chain,
The negro that drives the long dray of the stone-yard,
    steady and tall he stands pois'd on one leg on the
    string-piece,
His blue shirt exposes his ample neck and breast and
    loosens over his hip-band,
His glance is calm and commanding, he tosses the slouch
    of his hat away from his forehead,
The sun falls on his crispy hair and mustache, falls on the
    black of his polish'd and perfect limbs.

I behold the picturesque giant and love him, and I do not
    stop there,
I go with the team also.

In me the caresser of life wherever moving, backward as
    well as forward sluing,
To niches aside and junior bending, not a person or object
    missing,
Absorbing all to myself and for this song.

Oxen that rattle the yoke and chain or halt in the leafy
    shade, what is that you express in your eyes?
It seems to me more than all the print I have read in my
    life.

My tread scares the wood-drake and wood-duck on my dis-
    tant and day-long ramble,
They rise together, they slowly circle around.

I believe in those wing'd purposes,
And acknowledge red, yellow, white, playing within me,
And consider green and violet and the tufted crown inten-
    tional,
And do not call the tortoise unworthy because she is not
    something else,
And the jay in the woods never studied the gamut, yet
    trills pretty well to me,
And the look of the bay mare shames silliness out of me.

.   .   .   .   .

16

I am of old and young, of the foolish as much as the wise,
Regardless of others, ever regardful of others,
Maternal as well as paternal, a child as well as a man,

Stuff'd with the stuff that is coarse and stuff'd with the
    stuff that is fine,
One of the Nation of many nations, the smallest the same
    and the largest the same,
A Southerner soon as a Northerner, a planter nonchalant
    and hospitable down by the Oconee I live,
A Yankee bound my own way ready for trade, my joints
    the limberest joints on earth and the sternest joints
    on earth,
A Kentuckian walking the vale of the Elkhorn in my deer-
    skin leggings, a Louisianian or Georgian,
A boatman over lakes or bays or along coasts, a Hoosier,
    Badger, Buckeye;
At home on Kanadian snow-shoes or up in the bush, or
    with fishermen off Newfoundland,
At home in the fleet of ice-boats, sailing with the rest and
    tacking,
At home on the hills of Vermont or in the woods of Maine, .
    or the Texan ranch,
Comrade of Californians, comrade of free North-Western-
    ers, (loving their big proportions,)
. Comrade of raftsmen and coalmen, comrade of all who
    shake hands and welcome to drink and meat,
A learner with the simplest, a teacher of the thoughtfull-
    est,
A novice beginning yet experient of myriads of seasons,
Of every hue and caste am I, of every rank and religion,
A farmer, mechanic, artist, gentleman, sailor, quaker,
Prisoner, fancy-man, rowdy, lawyer, physician, priest.

I resist any thing better than my own diversity,
Breathe the air but leave plenty after me,
And am not stuck up, and am in my place.

(The moth and the fish-eggs are in their place,
The bright suns I see and the dark suns I cannot see are in
their place,
The palpable is in its place and the impalpable is in its
place.)

17

These are really the thoughts of all men in all ages and
lands, they are not original with me,
If they are not yours as much as mine they are nothing, or
next to nothing,
If they are not the riddle and the untying of the riddle they
are nothing,
If they are not just as close as they are distant they are
nothing.

This is the grass that grows wherever the land is and the
water is,
This the common air that bathes the globe.

21

I am the poet of the Body and I am the poet of the Soul,
The pleasures of heaven are with me and the pains of hell
are with me,
The first I graft and increase upon myself, the latter I translate into a new tongue.

I am the poet of the woman the same as the man,
And I say it is as great to be a woman as to be a man,
And I say there is nothing greater than the mother of men.

I chant the chant of dilation or pride,
We have had ducking and deprecating about enough,
I show that size is only development.

Have you outstript the rest? are you the President?
It is a trifle, they will more than arrive there every one, .
    and still pass on.

I am he that walks with the tender and growing night
I call to the earth and sea half-held by the night.

Press close bare-bosom'd night—press close magnetic nour-
    ishing night!
Night of south winds—night of the large few stars!
Still nodding night—mad naked summer night.

Smile O voluptuous cool-breath'd earth!
Earth of the slumbering and liquid trees!
Earth of departed sunset—earth of the mountains misty-
    topt!
Earth of the vitreous pour of the full moon just tinged with
    blue!
Earth of shine and dark mottling the tide of the river!
Earth of the limpid gray of clouds brighter and clearer for
    my sake!
Far-swooping elbow'd earth—rich apple-blossom'd earth!
Smile, for your lover comes.

Prodigal, you have given me love—therefore I to you give
    love!
O unspeakable passionate love.

.   .   .   .   .

23

Endless unfolding of words of ages!
And mine a word of the modern, the word En-Masse.

A word of the faith that never balks,
Here or henceforward it is all the same to me, I accept Time
    absolutely.

It alone is without flaw, it alone rounds and completes all,
That mystic baffling wonder alone completes all.

I accept Reality and dare not question it,
Materialism first and last imbuing.

Hurrah for positive science ! long live exact demonstration !
Fetch stonecrop mixt with cedar and branches of lilac,
This is the lexicographer, this the chemist, this made a
    grammar of the old cartouches,
These mariners put the ship through dangerous unknown
    seas,
This is the geologist, this works with the scalpel, and this
    is a mathematician.

Gentlemen, to you the first honors always !
Your facts are useful, and yet they are not my dwelling,
I but enter by them to an area of my dwelling.

Less the reminders of properties told my words,
And more the reminders they of life untold, and of freedom
    and extrication.

                .   .   .   .   .

                    32

I think I could turn and live with animals, they are so placid
    and self-contain'd,
I stand and look at them long and long.

They do not sweat and whine about their condition,
They do not lie awake in the dark and weep for their sins,

They do not make me sick discussing their duty to God,
Not one is dissatisfied, not one is demented with the mania
    of owning things,
Not one kneels to another, nor to his kind that lived thou-
    sands of years ago,
Not one is respectable or unhappy over the whole earth.

So they show their relations to me and I accept them,
They bring me tokens of myself, they evince them plainly
    in their possession.

I wonder where they get those tokens,
Did I pass that way huge times ago and negligently drop them?
Myself moving forward then and now and forever,
Gathering and showing more always and with velocity,
Infinite and omnigenous, and the like of these among them,
Not too exclusive toward the reachers of my remembrancers,
Picking out here one that I love, and now go with him on
    brotherly terms.

A gigantic beauty of a stallion, fresh and responsive to my
    caresses,
Head high in the forehead, wide between the ears,
Limbs glossy and supple, tail dusting the ground,
Eyes full of sparkling wickedness, ears finely cut, flexibly
    moving.

His nostrils dilate as my heels embrace him,
His well-built limbs tremble with pleasure as we race around
    and return.

I but use you a minute, then I resign you, stallion,
Why do I need your paces when I myself out-gallop them ?
Even as I stand or sit passing faster than you.

.   .   .   .   .

33

I understand the large hearts of heroes,
The courage of present times and all times,
How the skipper saw the crowded and rudderless wreck of
    the steam-ship, and Death chasing it up and down the
    storm,
How he knuckled tight and gave not back an inch, and was
    faithful of days and faithful of nights,
And chalk'd in large letters on a board, *Be of good cheer, we*
    will not desert you;
How he follow'd with them and tack'd with them three
    days and would not give it up,
How he saved the drifting company at last,
How the lank loose-gown'd women look'd when boated
    from the side of their prepared graves,
How the silent old-faced infants and the lifted sick, and the
    sharp-lipp'd unshaved men;
All this I swallow, it tastes good, I like it well, it becomes
    mine,
I am the man, I suffer'd, I was there.

The disdain and calmness of martyrs,
The mother of old, condemn'd for a witch, burnt with dry
    wood, her children gazing on,
The hounded slave that flags in the race, leans by the fence,
    blowing, cover'd with sweat,
The twinges that sting like needles his legs and neck, the
    murderous buckshot and the bullets,
All these I feel or am.

I am the hounded slave, I wince at the bite of the dogs,
Hell and despair are upon me, crack and again crack the
    marksmen,

I clutch the rails of the fence, my gore dribs, thinn'd with
    the ooze of my skin,
I fall on the weeds and stones,
The riders spur their unwilling horses, haul close,
Taunt my dizzy ears and beat me violently over the head
    with whip-stocks.

Agonies are one of my changes of garments,
I do not ask the wounded person how he feels, I myself be-
    come the wounded person,
My hurts turn livid upon me as I lean on a cane and observe.

I am the mash'd fireman with breast-bone broken,
Tumbling walls buried me in their debris,
Heat and smoke I inspired, I heard the yelling shouts of
    my comrades,
I heard the distant click of their picks and shovels,
They have clear'd the beams away, they tenderly lift me
    forth.

I lie in the night air in my red shirt, the pervading hush is
    for my sake,
Painless after all I lie exhausted but not so unhappy,
White and beautiful are the faces around me, the heads are
    bared of their fire-caps,
The kneeling crowd fades with the light of the torches.

Distant and dead resuscitate,
They show as the dial or move as the hands of me, I am
    the clock myself.

I am an old artillerist, I tell of my fort's bombardment,
I am there again.

Again the long roll of the drummers,
Again the attacking cannon, mortars,
Again to my listening ears the cannon responsive.

I take part, I see and hear the whole,
The cries, curses, roar, the plaudits for well-aim'd shots,
The ambulanza slowly passing trailing its red drip,
Workmen searching after damages, making indispensable
     repairs,
The fall of grenades through the rent roof, the fan-shaped
     explosion,
The whizz of limbs, heads, stone, wood, iron, high in the air.

Again gurgles the mouth of my dying general, he furiously
     waves with his hand,
He gasps through the clot *Mind not me—mind—the en-
     trenchments.*

          .   .   .   .   .

                        35

Would you hear of an old-time sea-fight?
Would you learn who won by the light of the moon and
     stars?
List to the yarn, as my grandmother's father the sailor told
     it to me.

Our foe was no skulk in his ship I tell you, (said he,)
His was the surly English pluck, and there is no tougher
     or truer, and never was, and never will be;
Along the lower'd eve he came horribly raking us.

We closed with him, the yards entangled, the cannon
     touch'd,
My captain lash'd fast with his own hands.

We had receiv'd some eighteen pound shots under the water.
On our lower-gun-deck two large pieces had burst at the first
    fire, killing all around and blowing up overhead.

Fighting at sun-down, fighting at dark,
Ten o'clock at night, the full moon well up, our leaks on
    the gain, and five feet of water reported,
The master-at-arms loosing the prisoners confined in the
    after-hold to give them a chance for themselves.

The transit to and from the magazine is now stopt by the
    sentinels,
They see so many strange faces they do not know whom to
    trust.

Our frigate takes fire,
The other asks if we demand quarter?
If our colors are struck and the fighting done?

Now I laugh content, for I hear the voice of my little
    captain,
We have not struck, he composedly cries, *we have just begun
    our part of the fighting.*

Only three guns are in use,
One is directed by the captain himself against the enemy's
    mainmast,
Two well serv'd with grape and canister silence his mus-
    ketry and clear his decks.

The tops alone second the fire of this little battery, espe-
    cially the main-top,
They hold out bravely during the whole of the action.

Not a moment's cease,
The leaks gain fast on the pumps, the fire eats toward the
    powder-magazine.

One of the pumps has been shot away, it is generally
    thought we are sinking.

Serene stands the little captain,
He is not hurried, his voice is neither high nor low,
His eyes give more light to us than our battle-lanterns.

Toward twelve there in the beams of the moon they sur-
    render to us.

.   .   .   .   .

40

To any one dying, thither I speed and twist the knob of
    the door,
Turn the bed-clothes toward the foot of the bed,
Let the physician and the priest go home.

I seize the descending man and raise him with resistless
    will,
O despairer, here is my neck,
By God, you shall not go down! hang your whole weight
    upon me.

I dilate you with tremendous breath, I buoy you up,
Every room of the house do I fill with an arm'd force,
Lovers of me, bafflers of graves.

Sleep—I and they keep guard all night,
Not doubt, not decease shall dare to lay finger upon you,

I have embraced you, and henceforth possess you to my-
    self,
And when you rise in the morning you will find what I tell
    you is so.

.   .   .   .   .

44

Long I was hugg'd close—long and long.

Immense have been the preparations for me,
Faithful and friendly the arms that have help'd me.

Cycles ferried my cradle, rowing and rowing like cheerful
    boatmen,
For room to me stars kept aside in their own rings,
They sent influences to look after what was to hold me.

Before I was born out of my mother generations guided
    me,
My embryo has never been torpid, nothing could overlay it.

For it the nebula cohered to an orb,
The long slow strata piled to rest it on,
Vast vegetables gave it sustenance,
Monstrous sauroids transported it in their mouths and de-
    posited it with care.

All forces have been steadily employ'd to complete and de-
    light me,
Now on this spot I stand with my robust soul.

.   .   .   .   .

.

45

Old age superbly rising! O welcome, ineffable grace of dy-
    ing days!

Every condition promulges not only itself, it promulges
    what grows after and out of itself,
And the dark hush promulges as much as any.

I open my scuttle at night and see the far-sprinkled sys-
    tems,
And all I see multiplied as high as I can cipher edge but
    the rim of the farther systems.

Wider and wider they spread, expanding, always expanding,
Outward and outward and forever outward.

My sun has his sun and round him obediently wheels,
He joins with his partners a group of superior circuit,
And greater sets follow, making specks of the greatest in-
    side them.

There is no stoppage and never can be stoppage,
If I, you, and the worlds, and all beneath or upon their
    surfaces, were this moment reduced back to a pallid
    float, it would not avail in the long run,
We should surely bring up again where we now stand,
And surely go as much farther, and then farther and
    farther.

A few quadrillions of eras, a few octillions of cubic leagues,
    do not hazard the span or make it impatient,
They are but parts, any thing is but a part.

See ever so far, there is limitless space outside of that,
Count ever so much, there is limitless time around that.

My rendezvous is appointed, it is certain,
The Lord will be there and wait till I come on perfect
    terms,
The great Camerado, the lover true for whom I pine will
    be there.

      .   .   .   .   .

48

I have said that the soul is not more than the body,
And I have said that the body is not more than the soul,
And nothing, not God, is greater to one than one's self is,
And whoever walks a furlong without sympathy walks to
    his own funeral drest in his shroud,
And I or you pocketless of a dime may purchase the pick
    of the earth,
And to glance with an eye or show a bean in its pod con-
    founds the learning of all times,
And there is no trade or employment but the young man
    following it may become a hero,
And there is no object so soft but it makes a hub for the
    wheel'd universe,
And I say to any man or woman, Let your soul stand cool
    and composed before a million universes.

And I say to mankind, Be not curious about God,
For I who am curious about each am not curious about God,
(No array of terms can say how much I am at peace about
    God and about death.)

I hear and behold God in every object, yet understand God
    not in the least,
Nor do I understand who there can be more wonderful than
    myself.

Why should I wish to see God better than this day?
I see something of God each hour of the twenty-four, and
    each moment then,
In the faces of men and women I see God, and in my own
    face in the glass,
I find letters from God dropt in the street, and every one is
    sign'd by God's name,
And I leave them where they are, for I know that where-
    soe'er I go,
Others will punctually come for ever and ever.

     .   .   .   .   .

51

The past and present wilt—I have fill'd them, emptied them,
And proceed to fill my next fold of the future.

Listener up there! what have you to confide to me?
Look in my face while I snuff the sidle of evening,
(Talk honestly, no one else hears you, and I stay only a
    minute longer.)

Do I contradict myself?
Very well then I contradict myself,
(I am large, I contain multitudes.)

I concentrate toward them that are nigh, I wait on the door-
    slab.

Who has done his day's work? who will soonest be through
    with his supper?
Who wishes to walk with me?

Will you speak before I am gone? will you prove already
    too late?

52

The spotted hawk swoops by and accuses me, he complains
    of my gab and my loitering.

I too am not a bit tamed, I too am untranslatable,
I sound my barbaric yawp over the roofs of the world.

The last scud of day holds back for me,
It flings my likeness after the rest and true as any on the
    shadow'd wilds,
It coaxes me to the vapor and the dusk.

I depart as air, I shake my white locks at the runaway sun,
I effuse my flesh in eddies, and drift it in lacy jags.

I bequeath myself to the dirt to grow from the grass I love,
If you want me again look for me under your boot-soles.

You will hardly know who I am or what I mean,
But I shall be good health to you nevertheless,
And filter and fibre your blood.

Failing to fetch me at first keep encouraged,
Missing me one place search another,
I stop somewhere waiting for you.

AT AUCTION

A MAN'S body at auction,
(For before the war I often go to the slave-mart and watch
    the sale,)
I help the auctioneer, the sloven does not half know his
    business.

Gentlemen look on this wonder,
Whatever the bids of the bidders they cannot be high
    enough for it,
For it the globe lay preparing quintillions of years without
    one animal or plant,
For it the revolving cycles truly and steadily roll'd.

In this head the all-baffling brain,
In it and below it the makings of heroes.

Examine these limbs, red, black, or white, they are cun-
    ning in tendon and nerve,
They shall be stript that you may see them.

Exquisite senses, life-lit eyes, pluck, volition,
Flakes of breast-muscle, pliant backbone and neck, flesh
    not flabby, good-sized arms and legs,
And wonders within there yet.

Within there runs blood,
The same old blood! the same red-running blood!
There swells and jets a heart, there all passions, desires,
    reachings, aspirations,
(Do you think they are not there because they are not ex-
    press'd in parlors and lecture-rooms?)

This is not only one man, this the father of those who
    shall be fathers in their turns,
In him the start of populous states and rich republics,
Of him countless immortal lives with countless embodi-
    ments and enjoyments.

How do you know who shall come from the offspring of
    his offspring through the centuries?
(Who might you find you have come from yourself, if you
    could trace back through the centuries?)

A woman's body at auction,
She too is not only herself, she is the teeming mother of
    mothers,
She is the bearer of them that shall grow and be mates to
    the mothers.

Have you ever loved the body of a woman?
Have you ever loved the body of a man?
Do you not see that these are exactly the same to all in all
    nations and times all over the earth?

If any thing is sacred the human body is sacred,
And the glory and sweet of a man is the token of manhood
    untainted,
And in man or woman a clean, strong, firm-fibred body, is
    more beautiful than the most beautiful face.

Have you seen the fool that corrupted his own live body?
    or the fool that corrupted her own live body?
For they do not conceal themselves, and cannot conceal
    themselves.

CALAMUS

WHOEVER YOU ARE HOLDING ME NOW IN HAND

WHOEVER you are holding me now in hand,
Without one thing all will be useless,
I give you fair warning before you attempt me further,
I am not what you supposed, but far different.

Who is he that would become my follower?
Who would sign himself a candidate for my affections?

The way is suspicious, the result uncertain, perhaps de-
    structive,
You would have to give up all else, I alone would expect
    to be your sole and exclusive standard,
Your novitiate would even then be long and exhausting,
The whole past theory of your life and all conformity to
    the lives around you would have to be abandon'd.
Therefore release me now before troubling yourself any
    further, let go your hand from my shoulders,
Put me down and depart on your way.

Or else by stealth in some wood for trial,
Or back of a rock in the open air,
(For in any roof'd room of a house I emerge not, nor in
    company,
And in libraries I lie as one dumb, a gawk, or unborn, or
    dead,)
But just possibly with you on a high hill, first watching
    lest any person for miles around approach unawares,

Or possibly with you sailing at sea, or on the beach of the
    sea or some quiet island,
Here to put your lips upon mine I permit you,
With the comrade's long-dwelling kiss or the new husband's
    kiss,
For I am the new husband and I am the comrade.

Or if you will, thrusting me beneath your clothing,
Where I may feel the throbs of your heart or rest upon
    your hip,
Carry me when you go forth over land or sea;
For thus merely touching you is enough, is best,
And thus touching you would I silently sleep and be car-
    ried eternally.

But these leaves conning you con at peril,
For these leaves and me you will not understand,
They will elude you at first and still more afterward, I will
    certainly elude you,
Even while you should think you had unquestionably
    caught me, behold !
Already you see I have escaped from you.

For it is not for what I have put into it that I have written
    this book,
Nor is it by reading it you will acquire it,
Nor do those know me best who admire me and vauntingly
    praise me,
Nor will the candidates for my love (unless at most a very
    few) prove victorious,
Nor will my poems do good only, they will do just as much
    evil, perhaps more,
For all is useless without that which you may guess at
    many times and not hit, that which I hinted at;
Therefore release me and depart on your way.

THE BASE OF ALL METAPHYSICS

And now gentlemen,
A word I give to remain in your memories and minds,
As base and finalè too for all metaphysics.

(So to the students the old professor,
At the close of his crowded course.)

Having studied the new and antique, the Greek and Ger-
    manic systems,
Kant having studied and stated, Fichte and Schelling and
    Hegel,
Stated the lore of Plato, and Socrates greater than Plato,
And greater than Socrates sought and stated, Christ divine
    having studied long,
I see reminiscent to-day those Greek and Germanic systems,
See the philosophies all, Christian churches and tenets see,
Yet underneath Socrates clearly see, and underneath Christ
    the divine I see,
The dear love of man for his comrade, the attraction of
    friend to friend,
Of the well-married husband and wife, of children and par-
    ents,
Of city for city and land for land.

WHEN I HEARD AT THE CLOSE OF THE DAY

When I heard at the close of the day how my name had been
    receiv'd with plaudits in the capitol, still it was not a
    happy night for me that follow'd,
And else when I carous'd, or when my plans were accom-
    plished, still I was not happy,

But the day when I rose at dawn from the bed of perfect
    health, refresh'd, singing, inhaling the ripe breath of
    autumn,
When I saw the full moon in the west grow pale and disap-
    pear in the morning light,
When I wander'd alone over the beach, and undressing
    bathed, laughing with the cool waters, and saw the sun
    rise,
And when I thought how my dear friend my lover was on
    his way coming, O then I was happy,
O then each breath tasted sweeter, and all that day my food
    nourish'd me more, and the beautiful day pass'd well,
And the next came with equal joy, and with the next at even-
    ing came my friend,
And that night while all was still I heard the waters roll
    slowly continually up the shores,
I heard the hissing rustle of the liquid and sands as directed
    to me whispering to congratulate me,
For the one I love most lay sleeping by me under the same
    cover in the cool night,
In the stillness in the autumn moonbeams his face was in-
    clined toward me,
And his arm lay lightly around my breast—and that night I
    was happy.

SALUT AU MONDE!

1

O TAKE my hand Walt Whitman !
Such gliding wonders ! such sights and sounds !
Such join'd unended links, each hook'd to the next,
Each answering all, each sharing the earth with all.

What widens within you Walt Whitman ?
What waves and soils exuding ?
What climes ? what persons and cities are here ?
Who are the infants, some playing, some slumbering ?
Who are the girls ? who are the married women ?
Who are the groups of old men going slowly with their
    arms about each other's necks ?
What rivers are these ? what forests and fruits are these ?
What are the mountains call'd that rise so high in the
    mists ?
What myriads of dwellings are they fill'd with dwellers ?

2

Within me latitude widens, longitude lengthens,
Asia, Africa, Europe, are to the east—America is provided
    for in the west,
Banding the bulge of the earth winds the hot equator,
Curiously north and south turn the axis-ends,
Within me is the longest day, the sun wheels in slanting
    rings, it does not set for months,
Stretch'd in due time within me the midnight sun just rises
    above the horizon and sinks again,

Within me zones, seas, cataracts, forests, volcanoes,
    groups,
Malaysia, Polynesia, and the great West Indian islands.

3

What do you hear Walt Whitman ?

I hear the workman singing and the farmer's wife singing,
I hear in the distance the sounds of children and of animals
    early in the day,
I hear emulous shouts of Australians pursuing the wild
    horse,
I hear the Spanish dance with castanets in the chestnut
    shade, to the rebeck and guitar,
I hear continual echoes from the Thames,
I hear fierce French liberty songs,
I hear of the Italian boat-sculler the musical recitative of
    old poems,
I hear the locusts in Syria as they strike the grain and
    grass with the showers of their terrible clouds,
I hear the Coptic refrain toward sundown, pensively fall-
    ing on the breast of the black venerable vast mother
    the Nile,
I hear the chirp of the Mexican muleteer, and the bells of
    the mule,
I hear the Arab muezzin calling from the top of the mosque,
I hear the Christian priests at the altars of their churches,
    I hear the responsive base and soprano,
I hear the cry of the Cossack, and the sailor's voice putting
    to sea at Okotsk,
I hear the wheeze of the slave-coffle as the slaves march
    on, as the husky gangs pass on by two and threes,
    fasten'd together with wrist-chains and ankle-chains,

I hear the Hebrew reading his records and psalms,
I hear the rhythmic myths of the Greeks, and the strong
    legends of the Romans,
I hear the tale of the divine life and bloody death of the
    beautiful God the Christ,
I hear the Hindoo teaching his favorite pupil the loves,
    wars, adages, transmitted safely to this day from poets
    who wrote three thousand years ago.

.   .   .   .   .

My spirit has pass'd in compassion and determination
    around the whole earth,
I have look'd for equals and lovers and found them ready
    for me in all lands,
I think some divine rapport has equalized me with them.

You vapors, I think I have risen with you, moved away to
    distant continents, and fallen down there, for reasons,
I think I have blown with you you winds;
You waters I have finger'd every shore with you,
I have run through what any river or strait of the globe
    has run through,
I have taken my stand on the bases of peninsulas and on
    the high embedded rocks, to cry thence:

Salut au monde!
What cities the light or warmth penetrates I penetrate
    those cities myself,
All islands to which birds wing their way I wing my way
    myself.

Toward you all, in America's name,
I raise high the perpendicular hand, I make the signal,
To remain after me in sight forever,
For all the haunts and homes of men.

CROSSING BROOKLYN FERRY

I

FLOOD-TIDE below me! I see you face to face!
Clouds of the west—sun there half an hour high—I see
    you also face to face.

Crowds of men and women attired in the usual costumes,
    how curious you are to me!
On the ferry-boats the hundreds and hundreds that cross,
    returning home, are more curious to me than you
    suppose,
And you that shall cross from shore to shore years hence
    are more to me, and more in my meditations, than
    you might suppose.

2

The impalpable sustenance of me from all things at all
    hours of the day,
The simple, compact, well-join'd scheme, myself disinte-
    grated, every one disintegrated yet part of the scheme,
The similitudes of the past and those of the future,
The glories strung like beads on my smallest sights and
    hearings, on the walk in the street and the passage
    over the river,
The current rushing so swiftly and swimming with me far
    away,
The others that are to follow me, the ties between me and
    them,
The certainty of others, the life, love, sight, hearing of
    others.

Others will enter the gates of the ferry and cross from
    shore to shore,
Others will watch the run of the flood-tide,
Others will see the shipping of Manhattan north and west,
    and the heights of Brooklyn to the south and east,
Others will see the islands large and small;
Fifty years hence, others will see them as they cross, the
    sun half an hour high,
A hundred years hence, or ever so many hundred years
    hence, others will see them,
Will enjoy the sunset, the pouring-in of the flood-tide, the
    falling-back to the sea of the ebb-tide.

3

It avails not, time nor place—distance avails not,
I am with you, you men and women of a generation, or
    ever so many generations hence,
Just as you feel when you look on the river and sky, so I
    felt,
Just as any of you is one of a living crowd, I was one of a
    crowd,
Just as you are refresh'd by the gladness of the river and
    the bright flow, I was refresh'd,
Just as you stand and lean on the rail, yet hurry with the
    swift current, I stood yet was hurried,
Just as you look on the numberless masts of ships and the
    thick-stemm'd pipes of steamboats, I look'd.

I too many and many a time cross'd the river of old,
Watched the Twelfth-month sea-gulls, saw them high in
    the air floating with motionless wings, oscillating their
    bodies,
Saw how the glistening yellow lit up parts of their bodies
    and left the rest in strong shadow,

Saw the slow-wheeling circles and the gradual edging tow-
    ard the south,
Saw the reflection of the summer sky in the water,
Had my eyes dazzled by the shimmering track of beams,
Look'd at the fine centrifugal spokes of light round the
    shape of my head in the sunlit water,
Look'd on the haze on the hills southward and south-west-
    ward,
Look'd on the vapor as it flew in fleeces tinged with violet,
Look'd toward the lower bay to notice the vessels arriving,
Saw their approach, saw aboard those that were near me,
Saw the white sails of schooners and sloops, saw the ships
    at anchor,
The sailors at work in the rigging or out astride the spars,
The round masts, the swinging motion of the hulls, the
    slender serpentine pennants,
The large and small steamers in motion, the pilots in their
    pilot-houses,
The white wake left by the passage, the quick tremulous
    whirl of the wheels,
The flags of all nations, the falling of them at sunset,
The scallop-edged waves in the twilight, the ladled cups,
    the frolicsome crests and glistening,
The stretch afar growing dimmer and dimmer, the gray
    walls of the granite storehouses by the docks,
On the river the shadowy group, the big steam-tug closely
    flank'd on each side by the barges, the hay-boat, the
    belated lighter,
On the neighboring shore the fires from the foundry chim-
    neys burning high and glaringly into the night,
Casting their flicker of black contrasted with wild red and
    yellow light over the tops of houses, and down into
    the clefts of streets.

4

These and all else were to me the same as they are to you,
I loved well those cities, loved well the stately and rapid
    river,
The men and women I saw were all near to me,
Others the same—others who look back on me because I
    look'd forward to them,
(The time will come, though I stop here to-day and to-night.)

5

What is it then between us?
What is the count of the scores or hundreds of years be-
    tween us?

Whatever it is, it avails not—distance avails not, and place
    avails not,
I too lived, Brooklyn of ample hills was mine,
I too walk'd the streets of Manhattan island, and bathed in
    the waters around it,
I too felt the curious abrupt questionings stir within me,
In the day among crowds of people sometimes they came
    upon me,
In my walks home late at night or as I lay in my bed they
    came upon me,
I too had been struck from the float forever held in solution,
I too had receiv'd identity by my body,
That I was I knew was of my body, and what I should be I
    knew I should be of my body.

6

It is not upon you alone the dark patches fall,
The dark threw its patches down upon me also,

The best I had done seem'd to me blank and suspicious,
My great thoughts as I supposed them, were they not in
    reality meagre?
Nor is it you alone who know what it is to be evil,
I am he who knew what it was to be evil,
I too knitted the old knot of contrariety,
Blabb'd, blush'd, resented, lied, stole, grudg'd,
Had guile, anger, lust, hot wishes I dared not speak,
Was wayward, vain, greedy, shallow, sly, cowardly, malig-
    nant,
The wolf, the snake, the hog, not wanting in me,
The cheating look, the frivolous word, the adulterous wish,
    not wanting,
Refusals, hates, postponements, meanness, laziness, none
    of these wanting,
Was one with the rest, the days and haps of the rest,
Was call'd by my nighest name by clear loud voices of
    young men as they saw me approaching or passing,
Felt their arms on my neck as I stood, or the negligent
    leaning of their flesh against me as I sat,
Saw many I loved in the street or ferry-boat or public as-
    sembly, yet never told them a word,
Lived the same life with the rest, the same old laughing,
    gnawing, sleeping,
Play'd the part that still looks back on the actor or actress,
The same old role, the role that is what we make it, as
    great as we like,
Or as small as we like, or both great and small.

7

Closer yet I approach you,
What thought you have of me now, I had as much of you—
    I laid in my stores in advance,
I consider'd long and seriously of you before you were born.

Who was to know what should come home to me ?
Who knows but I am enjoying this ?
Who knows, for all the distance, but I am as good as look-
   ing at you now, for all you cannot see me ?

                             8

Ah, what can ever be more stately and admirable to me than
      mast-hemm'd Manhattan ?
River and sunset and scallop-edg'd waves of flood-tide ?
The sea-gulls oscillating their bodies, the hay-boat in the
      twilight, and the belated lighter ?
What gods can exceed these that clasp me by the hand, and
      with voices I love call me promptly and loudly by my
      nighest name as I approach ?
What is more subtle than this which ties me to the woman
      or man that looks in my face ?
Which fuses me into you now, and pours my meaning into
      you ?

We understand then do we not ?
What I promis'd without mentioning it, have you not ac-
      cepted ?
What the study could not teach—what the preaching could
      not accomplish is accomplish'd, is it not ?

                             9

Flow on, river! flow with the flood-tide, and ebb with the
      ebb-tide!
Frolic on, crested and scallop-edg'd waves!
Gorgeous clouds of the sunset! drench with your splendor
      me, or the men and women generations after me!
Cross from shore to shore, countless crowds of passengers!

Stand up, tall masts of Mannahatta! stand up, beautiful
hills of Brooklyn!

Throb, baffled and curious brain! throw out questions and
answers!

Suspend here and everywhere, eternal float of solution!

Gaze, loving and thirsting eyes, in the house or street or
public assembly!

Sound out, voices of young men! loudly and musically call
me by my nighest name!

Live, old life! play the part that looks back on the actor or
actress!

Play the old role, the role that is great or small according
as one makes it!

Consider, you who peruse me, whether I may not in unknown ways be looking upon you;

Be firm, rail over the river, to support those who lean idly,
yet haste with the hasting current;

Fly on, sea-birds! fly sideways, or wheel in large circles
high in the air;

Receive the summer sky, you water, and faithfully hold it
till all downcast eyes have time to take it from you!

Diverge, fine spokes of light, from the shape of my head,
or any one's head, in the sunlit water!

Come on, ships from the lower bay! pass up or down,
white-sail'd schooners, sloops, lighters!

Flaunt away, flags of all nations! be duly lower'd at sunset!

Burn high your fires, foundry chimneys! cast black shadows
at nightfall! cast red and yellow light over the tops of
the houses!

Appearances, now or henceforth, indicate what you are,

You necessary film, continue to envelop the soul,

About my body for me, and your body for you, be hung
our divinest aromas,

Thrive, cities—bring your freight, bring your shows, ample
    and sufficient rivers,
Expand, being than which none else is perhaps more
    spiritual,
Keep your places, objects than which none else is more
    lasting.

You have waited, you always wait, you dumb, beautiful
    ministers,
We receive you with free sense at last, and are insatiate
    henceforward,
Not you any more shall be able to foil us, or withhold
    yourself from us,
We use you, and do not cast you aside—we plant you per-
    manently within us,
We fathom you not—we love you—there is perfection in
    you also,
You furnish your parts toward eternity,
Great or small you furnish your parts toward the soul.

FROM "SONG OF THE EXPOSITION"

AWAY with themes of war ! away with war itself !
Hence from my shuddering sight to never more return that
    show of blacken'd, mutilated corpses !
That hell unpent and raid of blood, fit for wild tigers or for
    lop-tongued wolves, not reasoning men,
And in its stead speed industry's campaigns,
With thy undaunted armies, engineering,
Thy pennants labor, loosen'd to the breeze,
Thy bugles sounding loud and clear.

Away with old romance !
Away with novels, plots and plays of foreign courts,
Away with love-verses sugar'd in rhyme, the intrigues,
    amours of idlers,
Fitted for only banquets of the night where dancers to late
    music slide,
The unhealthy pleasures, extravagant dissipations of the
    few,
With perfumes, heat and wine, beneath the dazzling chan-
    deliers.

To you ye reverent sane sisters,
I raise a voice for far superber themes for poets and for art,
To exalt the present and the real,
To teach the average man the glory of his daily walk and
    trade,
To sing in songs how exercise and chemical life are never
    to be baffled,
To manual work for each and all, to plough, hoe, dig,

To plant and tend the tree, the berry, vegetables, flowers,
For every man to see to it that he really do something, for
    every woman too;
To use the hammer and the saw, (rip, or cross-cut,)
To cultivate a turn for carpentering, plastering, painting,
To work as tailor, tailoress, nurse, hostler, porter,
To invent a little, something ingenious, to aid the washing,
    cooking, cleaning,
And hold it no disgrace to take a hand at them themselves.

I say I bring thee Muse to-day and here,
All occupations, duties broad and close,
Toil, healthy toil and sweat, endless, without cessation,
The old, old practical burdens, interests, joys,
The family, parentage, childhood, husband and wife,
The house-comforts, the house itself and all its belongings,
Food and its preservation, chemistry applied to it,
Whatever forms the average, strong, complete, sweet-
    blooded man or woman, the perfect longeve personality,
And helps its present life to health and happiness, and shapes
    its soul,
For the eternal real life to come.

With latest connections, works, the inter-transportation of
    the world,
Steam-power, the great express lines, gas, petroleum,
These triumphs of our time, the Atlantic's delicate cable,
The Pacific railroad, the Suez canal, the Mont Cenis and
    Gothard and Hoosac tunnels, the Brooklyn bridge,
This earth all spann'd with iron rails, with lines of steam-
    ships threading every sea,
Our own rondure, the current globe I bring.

A BROADWAY PAGEANT

I

OVER the Western sea hither from Niphon come,
Courteous, the swart-cheek'd two-sworded envoys,
Leaning back in their open barouches, bare-headed, im-
    passive,
Ride to-day through Manhattan.

Libertad! I do not know whether others behold what I be-
    hold,
In the procession along with the nobles of Niphon, the er-
    rand-bearers,
Bringing up the rear, hovering above, around, or in the
    ranks marching,
But I will sing you a song of what I behold Libertad.

When million-footed Manhattan unpent descends to her
    pavements,
When the thunder-cracking guns arouse me with the proud
    roar I love,
When the round-mouth'd guns out of the smoke and smell
    I love spit their salutes,
When the fire-flashing guns have fully alerted me, and
    heaven-clouds canopy my city with a delicate thin haze,
When gorgeous the countless straight stems, the forests at
    the wharves, thicken with colors,
When every ship richly drest carries her flag at the peak,

When pennants trail and street-festoons hang from the
    windows,
When Broadway is entirely given up to foot-passengers and
    foot-standers, when the mass is densest,)
When the façades of the houses are alive with people,when
    eyes gaze riveted tens of thousands at a time,
When the guests from the islands advance, when the pa-
    geant moves forward visible,
When the summons is made, when the answer that waited
    thousands of years answers,
I too arising, answering, descend to the pavements, merge
    with the crowd, and gaze with them.

2

Superb-faced Manhattan!
Comrade Americanos! to us, then at last the Orient comes.

To us, my city,
Where our tall-topt marble and iron beauties range on op-
    posite sides, to walk in the space between,
To-day our Antipodes comes.

The Originatress comes,
The nest of languages, the bequeather of poems, the race
    of eld,
Florid with blood, pensive, rapt with musings, hot with
    passion,
Sultry with perfume, with ample and flowing garments,
With sunburnt visage, with intense soul and glittering eyes,
The race of Brahma comes.

See my cantabile! these and more are flashing to us from
    the procession,
As it moves changing, a kaleidoscope divine it moves
    changing before us.

For not the envoys nor the tann'd Japanee from his island
    only,
Lithe and silent the Hindoo appears, the Asiatic continent
    itself appears, the past, the dead,
The murky night-morning of wonder and fable inscrutable,
The envelop'd mysteries, the old and unknown hive-bees,
The north, the sweltering south, eastern Assyria, the He-
    brews, the ancient of ancients,
Vast desolated cities, the gliding present, all of these and
    more are in the pageant procession.

Geography, the world, is in it,
The Great Sea, the brood of islands, Polynesia, the coast
    beyond,
The coast you henceforth are facing—you Libertad! from
    your Western golden shores,
The countries there with their populations, the millions
    en-masse are curiously here,
The swarming market-places, the temples with idols ranged
    along the sides or at the end, bonze, brahmin, and
    llama,
Mandarin, farmer, merchant, mechanic, and fisherman,
The singing-girl and the dancing-girl, the ecstatic persons,
    the secluded emperors,
Confucius himself, the great poets and heroes, the war-
    riors, the castes, all,
Trooping up, crowding from all directions, from the Altay
    mountains,
From Thibet, from the four winding and far-flowing rivers
    of China,
From the southern peninsulas and the demi-continental
    islands, from Malaysia,
These and whatever belongs to them palpable show forth
    to me, and are seiz'd by me,

And I am seiz'd by them, and friendlily held by them,
Till as here them all I chant, Libertad ! for themselves
    and for you.

For I too raising my voice join the ranks of this pageant,
I am the chanter, I chant aloud over the pageant,
I chant the world on my Western sea,
I chant copious the islands beyond, thick as stars in the
    sky,
I chant the new empire grander than any before, as in a
    vision it comes to me,
I chant America the mistress, I chant a greater supremacy,
I chant projected a thousand blooming cities yet in time on
    those groups of sea-islands,
My sail-ships and steam-ships threading the archipelagoes,
My stars and stripes fluttering in the wind,
Commerce opening, the sleep of ages having done its work,
    races reborn, refresh'd,
Lives, works resumed—the object I know not—but the old,
    the Asiatic renew'd as it must be,
Commencing from this day surrounded by the world.

3

And you Libertad of the world !
You shall sit in the middle well-pois'd thousands and thou-
    sands of years,
As to-day from one side the nobles of Asia come to you,
As to-morrow from the other side the queen of England
    sends her eldest son to you.
The sign is reversing, the orb is enclosed,
The ring is circled, the journey is done,
The box-lid is but perceptibly open'd, nevertheless the
    perfume pours copiously out of the whole box.

Young Libertad ! with the venerable Asia, the all-mother,
Be considerate with her now and ever hot Libertad, for
    you are all,
Bend your proud neck to the long-off mother now sending
    messages over the archipelagoes to you,
Bend your proud neck low for once, young Libertad.

Were the children straying westward so long? so wide the
    tramping?
Were the precedent dim ages debouching westward from
    Paradise so long?
Were the centuries steadily footing it that way, all the
    while unknown, for you, for reasons?

They are justified, they are accomplish'd, they shall now
    be turn'd the other way also, to travel toward you
    thence,
They shall now also march obediently eastward for your
    sake Libertad.

GIVE ME THE SPLENDID SILENT SUN

I

GIVE me the splendid silent sun with all his beams full-
    dazzling,
Give me juicy autumnal fruit ripe and red from the orchard,
Give me a field where the unmow'd grass grows,
Give me an arbor, give me the trellis'd grape,
Give me fresh corn and wheat, give me serene-moving ani-
    mals teaching content,
Give me nights perfectly quiet as on high plateaus west of
    the Mississippi, and I looking up at the stars,
Give me odorous at sunrise a garden of beautiful flowers
    where I can walk undisturb'd,
Give me for marriage a sweet-breath'd woman of whom I
    should never tire,
Give me a perfect child, give me away aside from the noise
    of the world a rural domestic life,
Give me to warble spontaneous songs recluse by myself,
    for my own ears only,
Give me solitude, give me Nature, give me again O Nature
    your primal sanities!

These demanding to have them, (tired with ceaseless ex-
    citement, and rack'd by the war-strife,)
These to procure incessantly asking, rising in cries from
    my heart,
While yet incessantly asking still I adhere to my city,
Day upon day and year upon year O city, walking your
    streets,

Where you hold me enchain'd a certain time refusing to
    give me up,
Yet giving to make me glutted, enrich'd of soul, you give
    me forever faces;
(O I see what I sought to escape, confronting, reversing
    my cries,
I see my own soul trampling down what it ask'd for.)

2

Keep your splendid silent sun,
Keep your woods O Nature, and the quiet places by the
    woods,
Keep your fields of clover and timothy, and your corn-fields
    and orchards,
Keep the blossoming buckwheat fields where the Ninth-
    month bees hum;
Give me faces and streets—give me these phantoms inces-
    sant and endless along the trottoirs!
Give me interminable eyes—give me women—give me
    comrades and lovers by the thousand!
Let me see new ones every day—let me hold new ones by
    the hand every day!
Give me such shows—give me the streets of Manhattan!
Give me Broadway, with the soldiers marching—give me
    the sound of the trumpets and drums!
(The soldiers in companies or regiments—some starting
    away, flush'd and reckless,
Some, their time up, returning with thinn'd ranks, young,
    yet very old, worn, marching, noticing nothing;)
Give me the shores and wharves heavy-fringed with black
    ships!
O such for me! O an intense life, full to repletion and
    varied!

The life of the theatre, bar-room, huge hotel, for me!
The saloon of the steamer! the crowded excursion for me!
    the torchlight procession!
The dense brigade bound for the war, with high piled mili-
    tary wagons following;
People, endless, streaming, with strong voices, passions,
    pageants,
Manhattan streets with their powerful throbs, with beating
    drums as now,
The endless and noisy chorus, the rustle and clank of mus-
    kets, (even the sight of the wounded,)
Manhattan crowds, with their turbulent musical chorus!
Manhattan faces and eyes forever for me.

THE OX-TAMER

IN a far-away northern county in the placid pastoral region,
Lives my farmer friend, the theme of my recitative, a
    famous tamer of oxen,
There they bring him the three-year-olds and the four-year-
    olds to break them,
He will take the wildest steer in the world and break him
    and tame him,
He will go fearless without any whip where the young
    bullock chafes up and down the yard,
The bullock's head tosses restless high in the air with raging
    eyes,
Yet see you ! how soon his rage subsides—how soon this
    tamer tames him;
See you ! on the farms hereabout a hundred oxen young
    and old, and he is the man who has tamed them,
They all know him, all are affectionate to him;
See you ! some are such beautiful animals, so lofty looking;
Some are buff-color'd, some mottled, one has a white line
    running along his back, some are brindled,
Some have wide flaring horns (a good sign)—see you ! the
    bright hides,
See, the two with stars on their foreheads—see, the round
    bodies and broad backs,
How straight and square they stand on their legs—what
    fine sagacious eyes !
How they watch their tamer—they wish him near them—
    how they turn to look after him !
What yearning expression ! how uneasy they are when he
    moves away from them;

Now I marvel what it can be he appears to them, (books,
    politics, poems, depart—all else departs,)
I confess I envy only his fascination—my silent, illiterate
    friend,
Whom a hundred oxen love there in his life on farms,
In the northern county far, in the placid pastoral region.

PROUD MUSIC OF THE STORM

1

PROUD music of the storm,
Blast that careers so free, whistling across the prairies,
Strong hum of forest tree-tops—wind of the mountains,
Personified dim shapes—you hidden orchestras,
You serenades of phantoms with instruments alert,
Blending with Nature's rhythmus all the tongues of nations;
You chords left as by vast composers—you choruses,
You formless, free, religious dances—you from the Orient,
You undertone of rivers, roar of pouring cataracts,
You sounds from distant guns with galloping cavalry,
Echoes of camps with all the different bugle-calls,
Trooping tumultuous, filling the midnight late, bending me
    powerless,
Entering my lonesome slumber-chamber, why have you
    seiz'd me?

2

Come forward O my soul, and let the rest retire,
Listen, lose not, it is toward thee they tend,
Parting the midnight, entering my slumber-chamber,
For thee they sing and dance O soul.
A festival song,
The duet of the bridegroom and the bride, a marriage-
    march,
With lips of love, and hearts of lovers fill'd to the brim with
    love,
The red-flush'd cheeks and perfumes, the cortege swarm-
    ing full of friendly faces young and old,
To flutes' clear notes and sounding harps' cantabile.

Now loud approaching drums,
Victoria ! see'st thou in powder-smoke the banners torn
    but flying ? the rout of the baffled ?
Hearest those shouts of a conquering army ?

(Ah soul, the sobs of women, the wounded groaning in
    agony,
The hiss and crackle of flames, the blacken'd ruins, the
    embers of cities,
The dirge and desolation of mankind.)

Now airs antique and mediæval fill me,
I see and hear old harpers with their warps at Welsh festi-
    vals,
I hear the minnesingers singing their lays of love,
I hear the minstrels, gleemen, troubadours, of the middle
    ages.

Now the great organ sounds,
Tremulous, while underneath, (as the hid footholds of the
    earth,
On which arising rest, and leaping forth depend,
All shapes of beauty, grace and strength, all hues we
    know,
Green blades of grass and warbling birds, children that
    gambol and play, the clouds of heaven above,)
The strong base stands, and its pulsations intermits not,
Bathing, supporting, merging all the rest, maternity of all
    the rest,
And with it every instrument in multitudes,
The players playing, all the world's musicians,
The solemn hymns and masses rousing adoration,
All passionate heart-chants, sorrowful appeals,
The measureless sweet vocalists of ages,

And for their solvent setting earth's own diapason,
Of winds and woods and mighty ocean waves,
A new composite orchestra, binder of years and climes, ten-
    fold renewer,
As of the far-back days the poets tell, the Paradiso,
The straying thence, the separation long, but now the wan-
    dering done,
The journey done, the journeyman come home,
And man and art with Nature fused again.

Tutti ! for earth and heaven;
(The Almighty leader now for once has signal'd with his
    wand.)

The manly strophe of the husbands of the world,
And all the wives responding.

The tongues of violins,
(I think O tongues ye tell this heart, that cannot tell itself,
This brooding, yearning heart, that cannot tell itself.)

3

Ah from a little child,
Thou knowest soul how to me all sounds became music,
My mother's voice in lullaby or hymn,
(The voice, O tender voices, memory's loving voices,
Last miracle of all, O dearest mother's, sister's, voices;)
The rain, the growing corn, the breeze among the long-
    leav'd corn,
The measur'd sea-surf beating on the sand,
The twittering bird, the hawk's sharp scream,
The wild-fowl's notes at night as flying low migrating north
    or south,

The psalm in the country church or mid the clustering trees,
    the open air camp-meeting,
The fiddler in the tavern, the glee, the long-strung sailor-
    song,
The lowing cattle, bleating sheep, the crowing cock at
    dawn.

All songs of current lands come sounding round me,
The German airs of friendship, wine and love,
Irish ballads, merry jigs and dances, English warbles,
Chansons of France, Scotch tunes, and o'er the rest,
Italia's peerless compositions.

Across the stage with pallor on her face, yet lurid passion,
Stalks Norma brandishing the dagger in her hand.

I see poor crazed Lucia's eyes' unnatural gleam,
Her hair down her back falls loose and dishevel'd.

I see where Ernani walking the bridal garden,
Amid the scent of night-roses, radiant, holding his bride by
    the hand,
Hears the infernal call, the death-pledge of the horn.

To crossing swords and gray hairs bared to heaven,
The clear electric base and baritone of the world,
The trombone duo, Libertad forever!

From Spanish chestnut trees' dense shade,
By old and heavy convent walls a wailing song,
Song of lost love, the torch of youth and life quench'd in
    despair,
Song of the dying swan, Fernando's heart is breaking.

Awaking from her woes at last retriev'd Amina sings,
Copious as stars and glad as morning light the torrents of
    her joy.

(The teeming lady comes,
The lustrious orb, Venus contralto, the blooming mother,
Sister of loftiest gods, Alboni's self I hear.)

4

I hear those odes, symphonies, operas,
I hear in the *William Tell* the music of an arous'd and angry
    people,
I hear Meyerbeer's *Huguenots*, the *Prophet*, or *Robert*,
Gounod's *Faust*, or Mozart's *Don Juan*.

I hear the dance-music of all nations,
The waltz, some delicious measure, lapsing, bathing me in
    bliss,
The bolero to tinkling guitars and clattering castanets.

I see religious dances old and new,
I hear the sound of the Hebrew lyre,
I see the crusaders marching bearing the cross on high, to
    the martial clang of cymbals,
I hear dervishes monotonously chanting, interspers'd with
    frantic shouts, as they spin around turning always
    towards Mecca,
I see the rapt religious dances of the Persians and the Arabs,
Again, at Eleusis, home of Ceres, I see the modern Greeks
    dancing,
I hear them clapping their hands as they bend their bodies,
I hear the metrical shuffling of their feet.

I see again the wild old Corybantian dance, the performers
    wounding each other,
I see the Roman youth to the shrill sound of flageolets
    throwing and catching their weapons,
As they fall on their knees and rise again.

I hear from the Mussulman mosque the muezzin calling,
I see the worshippers within, nor form nor sermon, argu-
    ment nor word,
But silent, strange, devout, rais'd, glowing heads, ecstatic
    faces.
I hear the Egyptian harp of many strings,
The primitive chants of the Nile boatmen,
The sacred imperial hymns of China,
To the delicate sounds of the king, (the stricken wood and
    stone,)
Or to Hindu flutes and the fretting twang of the vina,
A band of bayaderes.

5

Now Asia, Africa leave me, Europe seizing inflates me,
To organs huge and bands I hear as from vast concourses
    of voices,
Luther's strong hymn *Eine feste Burg ist unser Gott*,
Rossini's *Stabat Mater dolorosa*,
Or floating in some high cathedral dim with gorgeous col-
    or'd windows,
The passionate *Agnus Dei* or *Gloria in Excelsis*.

Composers ! mighty maestros !
And you, sweet singers of old lands, soprani, tenori, bassi !
To you a new bard caroling in the West,
Obeisant sends his love.

(Such led to thee O soul,
All senses, shows and objects, lead to thee,
But now it seems to me sound leads o'er all the rest.)

I hear the annual singing of the children in St. Paul's cathe-
    dral,
Or, under the high roof of some colossal hall, the sympho-
    nies, oratorios of Beethoven, Handel, or Haydn,
The *Creation* in billows of Godhood laves me.

Give me to hold all sounds, (I madly struggling cry,)
Fill me with all the voices of the universe,
Endow me with their throbbings, Nature's also,
The tempests, waters, winds, operas and chants, marches
    and dances,
Utter, pour in, for I would take them all !

6

Then I woke softly,
And pausing, questioning awhile the music of my dream,
And questioning all those reminiscences, the tempest in its
    fury,
And all the songs of sopranos and tenors,
And those rapt oriental dances of religious fervor,
And the sweet varied instruments, and the diapason of
    organs,
And all the artless plaints of love and grief and death,
I said to my silent curious soul out of the bed of the slum-
    ber-chamber,
Come, for I have found the clew I sought so long,
Let us go forth refresh'd amid the day,
Cheerfully tallying life, walking the world, the real,
Nourish'd henceforth by our celestial dream.

And I said, moreover,
Haply what thou hast heard O soul was not the sound of
winds,
Nor dream of raging storm, nor sea-hawk's flapping wings
nor harsh scream,
Nor vocalism of sun-bright Italy,
Nor German organ majestic, nor vast concourse of voices,
nor layers of harmonies,
Nor strophes of husbands and wives, nor sound of march-
ing soldiers,
Nor flutes, nor harps, nor the bugle-calls of camps,
But to a new rhythmus fitted for thee,
Poems bridging the way from Life to Death, vaguely
wafted in night air, uncaught, unwritten,
Which let us go forth in the bold day and write.

O VAST RONDURE

O VAST Rondure, swimming in space,
Cover'd all over with visible power and beauty,
Alternate light and day and the teeming spiritual darkness,
Unspeakable high processions of sun and moon and count-
    less stars above,
Below, the manifold grass and waters, animals, mountains,
    trees,
With inscrutable purpose, some hidden prophetic intention,
Now first it seems my thought begins to span thee.

Down from the gardens of Asia descending radiating,
Adam and Eve appear, then their myriad progeny after
    them,
Wandering, yearning, curious, with restless explorations,
With questionings, baffled, formless, feverish, with never-
    happy hearts,
With that sad incessant refrain, *Wherefore unsatisfied soul?*
    and *Whither O mocking life?*

Ah who shall soothe these feverish children?
Who justify these restless explorations?
Who speak the secret of impassive earth?
Who bind it to us? what is this separate Nature so unnat-
    ural?
What is this earth to our affections? (unloving earth, with-
    out a throb to answer ours,
Cold earth, the place of graves.)

Yet soul be sure the first intent remains, and shall be car-
　　ried out,
Perhaps even now the time has arrived.

After the seas are all cross'd, (as they seem already
　　cross'd,)
After the great captains and engineers have accomplish'd
　　their work,
After the noble inventors, after the scientists, the chemist.
　　the geologist, ethnologist,
Finally shall come the poet worthy that name,
The true son of God shall come singing his songs.

THE RED SQUAW

Now what my mother told me one day as we sat at dinner
  together,
Of when she was a nearly grown girl living home with her
  parents on the old homestead.

A red squaw came one breakfast-time to the old homestead,
On her back she carried a bundle of rushes for rush-bottom-
  ing chairs,
Her hair, straight, shiny, coarse, black, profuse, half-en·
  velop'd her face,
Her step was free and elastic, and her voice sounded ex-
  quisitely as she spoke.

My mother look'd in delight and amazement at the stranger,
She look'd at the freshness of her tall-borne face and full
  and pliant limbs,
The more she look'd upon her she loved her,
Never before had she seen such wonderful beauty and
  purity,
She made her sit on a bench by the jamb of the fireplace,
  she cook'd food for her,
She had no work to give her, but she gave her remem-
  brance and fondness.

The red squaw staid all the forenoon, and toward the mid-
  dle of the afternoon she went away,
O my mother was loth to have her go away,
All the week she thought of her, she watch'd for her many
  a month,
She remember'd her many a winter and many a summer,
But the red squaw never came nor was heard of there
  again.

AN OLD STAGE-DRIVER

A REMINISCENCE of the vulgar fate,
A frequent sample of the life and death of workmen,
Each after his kind.

Cold dash of waves at the ferry-wharf, posh and ice in the
  river, half-frozen mud in the streets,
A gray discouraged sky overhead, the short last daylight
  of December,
A hearse and stages, the funeral of an old Broadway stage-
  driver, the cortege mostly drivers.

Steady the trot to the cemetery, duly rattles the death-bell,
The gate is pass'd, the new-dug grave is halted at, the
  living alight, the hearse uncloses,
The coffin is pass'd out, lower'd and settled, the whip is
  laid on the coffin, the earth is swiftly shovel'd in,
The mound above is flatted with the spades—silence,
A minute—no one moves or speaks—it is done,
He is decently put away—is there any thing more?

He was a good fellow, free-mouth'd, quick-temper'd, not
  bad-looking,
Ready with life or death for a friend, fond of women,
  gambled, ate hearty, drank hearty,
Had known what it was to be flush, grew low-spirited toward the last, sicken'd, was help'd by a contribution,
Died, aged forty-one years—and that was his funeral.

Thumb extended, finger uplifted, apron, cape, gloves, strap,
    wet-weather clothes, whip carefully chosen,
Boss, spotter, starter, hostler, somebody loafing on you,
    you loafing on somebody, headway, man before and
    man behind,
Good day's work, bad day's work, pet stock, mean stock,
    first out, last out, turning-in at night,
To think that these are so much and so nigh to other
    drivers, and he there takes no interest in them.

MANNAHATTA

I was asking for something specific and perfect for my city,
Whereupon lo! upsprang the aboriginal name.

Now I see what there is in a name, a word, liquid, sane,
    unruly, musical, self-sufficient,
I see that the word of my city is that word from of old,
Because I see that word nested in nests of water-bays,
    superb,
Rich, hemm'd thick all around with sailships and steam-
    ships, an island sixteen miles long, solid-founded,
Numberless crowded streets, high growths of iron, slender,
    strong, light, splendidly uprising toward clear skies,
Tides swift and ample, well-loved by me, toward sundown,
The flowing sea-currents, the little islands, larger adjoining
    islands, the heights, the villas,
The countless masts, the white shore-steamers, the lighters,
    the ferry-boats, the black sea-steamers well-model'd,
The down-town streets, the jobbers' houses of business,
    the houses of business of the ship-merchants and money-
    brokers, the river-streets,
Immigrants arriving, fifteen or twenty thousand in a week,
The carts hauling goods, the manly race of drivers of
    horses, the brown-faced sailors,
The summer air, the bright sun shining, and the sailing
    clouds aloft,
The winter snows, the sleigh-bells, the broken ice in the
    river, passing along up or down with the flood-tide or
    ebb-tide,

The mechanics of the city, the masters, well-form'd, beau-
    tiful-faced, looking you straight in the eyes,
Trottoirs throng'd, vehicles, Broadway, the women, the
    shops and shows,
A million people—manners free and superb—open voices—
    hospitality—the most courageous and friendly young
    men,
City of hurried and sparkling waters! city of spires and
    masts!
City nested in bays! my city!

AFTER AN INTERVAL

(Nov. 22, 1875, Midnight—Saturn and Mars in conjunction)

AFTER an interval, reading, here in the midnight,
With the great stars looking on—all the stars of Orion
    looking,
And the silent Pleiades—and the duo looking of Saturn and
    ruddy Mars;
Pondering, reading my own songs, after a long interval,
    (sorrow and death familiar now,)
Ere closing the book, what pride! what joy! to find them,
Standing so well the test of death and night!
And the duo of Saturn and Mars!

SO LONG !

CAMERADO, this is no book,
Who touches this touches a man,
(Is it night ? are we here together alone ?)
It is I you hold and who holds you,
I spring from the pages into your arms—decease calls me
    forth.

O how your fingers drowse me,
Your breath falls around me like dew, your pulse lulls the
    tympans of my ears,
I feel immerged from head to foot,
Delicious, enough.

Enough O deed impromptu and secret,
Enough O gliding present—enough O summ'd-up past.

Dear friend whoever you are take this kiss,
I give it especially to you, do not forget me,
I feel like one who has done work for the day to retire
    awhile,
I receive now again of my many translations, from my ava-
    taras ascending, while others doubtless await me,
An unknown sphere more real than I dream'd, more direct,
    darts awakening rays about me, *So long !*
Remember my words, I may again return,
I love you, I depart from materials,
I am as one disembodied, triumphant, dead.

GOOD-BYE MY FANCY!

GOOD-BYE MY FANCY!

GOOD-BYE my Fancy!
Farewell dear mate, dear love!
I'm going away, I know not where,
Or to what fortune, or whether I may ever see you again,
So Good-bye my Fancy.

Now for my last—let me look back a moment;
The slower fainter ticking of the clock is in me,
Exit, nightfall, and soon the heart-thud stopping.

Long have we lived, joy'd, caress'd together;
Delightful!—now separation—Good-bye my Fancy.

Yet let me not be too hasty,
Long indeed have we lived, slept, filter'd, become really
    blended into one;
Then if we die we die together, (yes, we'll remain one,)
If we go anywhere we'll go together to meet what happens,
May-be we'll be better off and blither, and learn something,
May-be it is yourself now really ushering me to the true
    songs, (who knows?)
May-be it is you the mortal knob really undoing, turning—
    so now finally,
Good-bye—and hail! my Fancy.

Price-List of Publications issued by

CHARLES L. WEBSTER & CO.

William Sharp.

Flower o' the Vine: Romantic Ballads and Sospiri di Roma.—This volume contains the poems in Mr. Sharp's latest books of verse, now entirely out of print. His collaboration with Blanche Willis Howard in the novel "A Fellowe and His Wife," has made his name familiar to American readers. As one of the most popular of the younger English poets, we anticipate an equal success in America for "Flower o' the Vine," for which Mr. Thomas A. Janvier has prepared an Introduction. Handsomely bound, uniform with Aldrich's "Sisters' Tragedy" and Cora Fabbri's "Lyrics." Cloth, $1.50.

Dan Beard.

Moonblight and Three Feet of Romance.—Octavo, 300 pages, fully illustrated. This story we believe will take rank with "Looking Backward." It treats of some of the great social problems of the day in a novel, powerful, and intensely interesting manner. The hero becomes strangely endowed with the power of seeing people in their true light. It is needless to say that this power proves both a curse and a blessing, and leads to many and strange adventures. Mr. Beard's reputation as an artist is world-wide, and the numerous illustrations he provides for this book powerfully portray the spirit of the text. Cloth, ink and gold stamps, $1.00.

Mark Twain's Books.

Adventures of Huckleberry Finn.—Holiday edition. Square 8vo, 366 pages. Illustrated by E. W. Kemble. Sheep, $3.25; cloth, $2.75.

New Cheap Edition of Huckleberry Finn.—12mo, 318 pages, with a few illustrations. Cloth, $1.00.

The Prince and the Pauper.—A square 8vo volume of 411 pages. Beautifully illustrated. Sheep $3.75; cloth, $3.00.

A Connecticut Yankee in King Arthur's Court.—A square 8vo of 575 pages; 221 illustrations by Dan Beard. Half morocco, $5.00; sheep, $4.00; cloth, $3.00.

Mark Twain Holiday Set.—Three volumes in a box, consisting of the best editions of "Huckleberry Finn," "Prince and Pauper," and "A Connecticut Yankee." Square 8vo. Uniform in size, binding, and color. Sold only in sets. Cloth, $6.00.

Eighteen Short Stories and Sketches.—By Mark Twain. Including "The Stolen White Elephant," "Some Rambling Notes," "The Carnival of Crime," "A Curious Experience," "Punch, Brothers, Punch," "The Invalid's Story," etc., etc. 16mo, 306 pages. Cloth, $1.00.

Mark Twain's "Library of Humor."—A volume of 145 Characteristic Selections from the Best Writers, together with a Short Biographical Sketch of Each Author quoted. Compiled by Mark Twain. Nearly 200 illustrations by E. W Kemble. 8vo, 707 pages. Full Turkey morocco, $7.00; half morocco, $5.00; half seal, $4.25; sheep, $4.00; cloth, $3.50.

Life on the Mississippi.—8vo, 624 pages; and over 300 illustrations. Sheep, $4.25; cloth, $3.50.

Innocents Abroad; or, The New Pilgrim's Progress. Sheep, $4.00; cloth, $3.50.

Roughing It.—600 pages; 300 illustrations. Sheep, $4.00; cloth, $3.50.

Sketches, Old and New.—320 pages; 122 illustrations. Sheep, $3.50; cloth, $3.00.

Adventures of Tom Sawyer.—150 engravings; 275 pages. Sheep, $3.25; cloth, $2.75.

The Gilded Age.—576 pages; 212 illustrations. Sheep, $4.00; cloth, $3.50.

A Tramp Abroad. Mark Twain in Europe.—A Companion Volume to "Innocents Abroad." 631 pages. Sheep, $4.00; cloth, $3.50.

Charles L. Webster & Co.

The War Series.

The Genesis of the Civil War.—The Story of Sumter, by Major-General S. W. Crawford, A. M., M. D., LL. D. Illustrated with steel and wood engravings and fac-similes of celebrated letters. 8vo, uniform with Grant's Memoirs. Full morocco, $8.00; half morocco, $5.50; sheep, $4.25; cloth, $3.50.

Personal Memoirs of General Grant.—Illustrations and maps, etc. 2 vols.; 8vo. Half morocco, per set, $11.00; sheep, per set, $6.00; cloth, per set, $7.00. A few sets in full Turkey morocco and tree calf for sale at special low prices.

Personal Memoirs of General Sherman.—With appendix by Hon. James G. Blaine. Illustrated; 2 vols.; 8vo, uniform with Grant's Memoirs. Half morocco, per set, $8.50; sheep, per set, $7.00; cloth, per set, $5.00. Cheap edition, in one large volume. Cloth, $2.00.

Personal Memoirs of General Sheridan.—Illustrated with steel portraits and woodcuts; 26 maps; 2 vols.; 8vo, uniform with Grant's Memoirs. Half morocco, per set, $10.00; sheep, per set, $8.00; cloth, per set, $6.00. A few sets in full Turkey morocco and tree calf to be disposed of at very low figures. Cheap edition, in one large volume, cloth binding, $2.00.

McClellan's Own Story.—With illustrations from sketches drawn on the field of battle by A. R. Wand, the Great War Artist. 8vo, uniform with Grant's Memoirs. Full morocco, $9.00; half morocco, $6.00; sheep, $4.75; cloth, $3.75.

Memoirs of John A. Dahlgren.—Rear-Admiral United States Navy. By his widow, Madeleine Vinton Dahlgren. A large octavo volume of 660 pages, with steel portrait, maps and illustrations. Cloth, $3.00.

Reminiscences of Winfield Scott Hancock.—By his wife. Illustrated; steel portraits of General and Mrs. Hancock; 8vo, uniform with Grant's Memoirs. Full morocco, $5.00; half morocco, $4.00; sheep, $3.50; cloth, $2.75.

Tenting on the Plains. — With the Life of General Custer, by Mrs. E. B. Custer. Illustrated; 8vo, uniform with Grant's Memoirs. Full morocco, $7.00; half morocco, $5.50; sheep, $4.25; cloth, $3.50.

Portrait of General Sherman. — A magnificent line etching on copper; size 19x24 inches; by the celebrated artist, Charles B. Hall. $2.00. (Special prices on quantities.)

The Great War Library. — Consisting of the best editions of the foregoing seven publications (Grant, Sheridan, Sherman, Hancock, McClellan, Custer and Crawford). Ten volumes in a box; uniform in style and binding. Half morocco, $50.00; sheep, $40.00; cloth, $30.00.

Other Biographical Works.

Life of Jane Welsh Carlyle. — By Mrs. Alexander Ireland. With portrait and fac-simile letter; 8vo, 324 pages. Vellum cloth, gilt top, $1.75.

Life and Letters of Roscoe Conkling. — By Hon. Alfred R. Conkling, Ph. B., LL.D.; steel portrait and fac-similes of important letters to Conkling from Grant, Arthur, Garfield, etc. 8vo, over 700 pages. Half morocco, $5.50; full seal, $5.00; sheep, $4.00; cloth, $3.00.

Life of Pope Leo XIII. — By Bernard O'Reilly, D. D., L. D. (Laval.) Written with the encouragement and blessing of His Holiness, the Pope. 8vo, 635 pages; colored and steel plates, and full-page illustrations. Half morocco, $6.00; half Russia, $5.00; cloth, gilt edges, $3.75.

Distinguished American Lawyers. — With their Struggles and Triumphs in the Forum. Containing an elegantly engraved portrait, autograph and biography of each subject, embracing the professional work and the public career of those called to serve their country. By Henry W. Scott. Introduction by Hon. John J. Ingalls. A large royal octavo volume of 716 pages, with 62 portraits of the most eminent lawyers. Sheep, $4.25; cloth, $3.50.

Miscellaneous.

Concise Cyclopedia of Religious Knowledge.—
Biblical, Biographical, Theological, Historical and Practical; edited by Rev. E. B. Sanford, M. A., assisted by
over 30 of the most eminent religious scholars in the
country. 1 vol.; royal 8vo, nearly 1,000 double-column
pages. Half morocco, $6.00; sheep, $5.00; cloth,
$3.50.

The Table.—How to Buy Food, How to Cook It, and
How to Serve It, by A. Filippini, of Delmonico's; the
only cook-book ever endorsed by Delmonico; contains
three menus for each day in the year, and over 1,500
original recipes, the most of which have been guarded
as secrets by the *chefs* of Delmonico. Contains the simplest as well as the most elaborate recipes. Presenta-
tion edition in full seal Russia, $4.50; Kitchen edition
in oil-cloth, $2.50.

One Hundred Ways of Cooking Eggs.—Mr. Filippini is probably the only man who can cook eggs in a
hundred different ways, and this little book will be
worth its price ten times over to any purchaser. Cloth
binding, ink and gold stamps, 50 cents.
Also uniform with the above,

**One Hundred Recipes for Cooking and Serving
Fish.**—This book contains only the best recipes, all of
which have been tested by Mr. Filippini during 25
years' experience with the Delmonicos. Cloth binding,
ink and gold stamps, 50 cents.

Yale Lectures on Preaching, and other Writings, by
Rev. Nathaniel Burton, D. D.; edited by Richard E.
Burton. 8vo, 640 pages; steel portrait. Cloth, $3.75.

Legends and Myths of Hawaii.—By the late King
Kalakaua; two steel portraits and 25 other illustrations.
8vo, 530 pages. Cloth, $3.00.

The Diversions of a Diplomat in Turkey.—By
the late Hon. S. S. Cox. 8vo, 685 pages; profusely
illustrated. Half morocco, $6.00; sheep, $4.75; cloth,
$3.75.

Inside the White House in War Times.—By W.
O. Stoddard, one of Lincoln's Private Secretaries.
12mo, 244 pages. Cloth, $1.00.

Tinkletop's Crime, and eighteen other Short Stories, by George R. Sims. 1 vol.; 12mo, 316 pages. Cloth, $1.00; paper covers, 50 cents.

My Life with Stanley's Rear Guard.—By Herbert Ward, one of the Captains of Stanley's Rear Guard; includes Mr. Ward's Reply to H. M. Stanley. 12mo. Cloth, $1.00; paper covers, 50 cents.

The Peril of Oliver Sargent.—By Edgar Janes Bliss. 12mo. Cloth, $1.00; paper covers, 50 cents.

The Old Devil and the Three Little Devils; or, Ivan The Fool, by Count Leo Tolstoi, translated direct from the Russian by Count Norraikow, with illustrations by the celebrated Russian artist, Gribayédoff. 12mo. Cloth, $1.00.

Life IS Worth Living, and Other Stories.— Translated direct from the Russian by Count Norraikow. This work, unlike some of his later writings, shows the great Russian at his best. The stories are pure, simple and powerful; intensely interesting as mere creations of fancy, but, like all Tolstoi's works, written for a purpose, and containing abundant food for earnest reflection. Cloth, ink and gold stamps, $1.00.

The Happy Isles, and Other Poems, by S. H. M. Byers. Small 12mo. Cloth binding, $1.00.

Physical Beauty: How to Obtain and How to Preserve It, by Annie Jenness Miller; including chapters on Hygiene, Foods, Sleep, Bodily Expression, the Skin, the Eyes, the Teeth, the Hair, Dress, the Cultivation of Individuality, etc., etc. An octavo volume of about 300 pages. Cloth, $2.00.

Hour-Glass Series.—By Daniel B. Lucas, LL. D., and J. Fairfax McLaughlin, LL. D. The first volume, which is now ready, contains a series of historical epitomes of national interest, with interesting sketches of such men as Henry Clay, Daniel O'Connell and Fisher Ames. Large 12mo. Cloth, $1.00.

Adventures of A Fair Rebel.—Author of "'Zeki'l," "Bet Crow," "S'phiry Ann," "Was It an Exceptional Case?" etc. A story that is sure to be eagerly sought after and read by Miss Crim's many admirers. Stamped cloth, $1.00; paper covers, 50 cents.

Printed in the United States
122199LV00005B/129/A